EASY PIANO

Taylor Swift
Speak Now

D1538110

ISBN 978-1-4584-0015-4

HAL•LEONARD®
CORPORATION

7777 W. BLUEMOUND RD. P.O. BOX 13819 MILWAUKEE, WI 53213

For all works contained herein:
Unauthorized copying, arranging, adapting, recording, Internet posting, public performance,
or other distribution of the printed music in this publication is an infringement of copyright.
Infringers are liable under the law.

Visit Hal Leonard Online at
www.halleonard.com

MINE

Words and Music by
TAYLOR SWIFT

Copyright © 2010 Sony/ATV Music Publishing LLC and Taylor Swift Music
All Rights Administered by Sony/ATV Music Publishing LLC, 8 Music Square West, Nashville, TN 37203
International Copyright Secured   All Rights Reserved

5

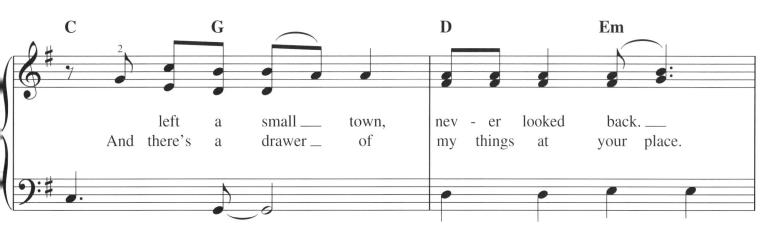

C   G   D   Em

left   a   small __ town,   nev - er   looked   back. __
And   there's   a   drawer _ of   my   things   at   your   place.

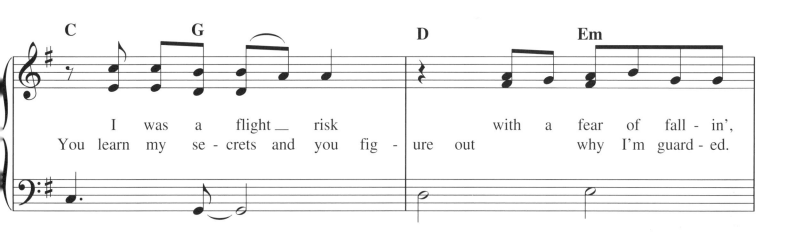

C   G   D   Em

I   was   a   flight __ risk   with   a   fear   of   fall - in',
You   learn   my   se - crets   and   you   fig - ure   out   why   I'm   guard - ed.

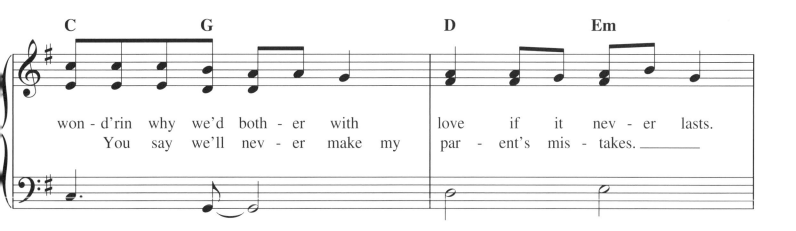

C   G   D   Em

won - d'rin   why   we'd   both - er   with   love   if   it   nev - er   lasts.
You   say   we'll   nev - er   make   my   par - ent's   mis - takes. _____

Csus2   G   D5   Csus2   G   D

I   say, __ "Can   you   be - lieve _ it?"
But   we   got   bills   to   pay;

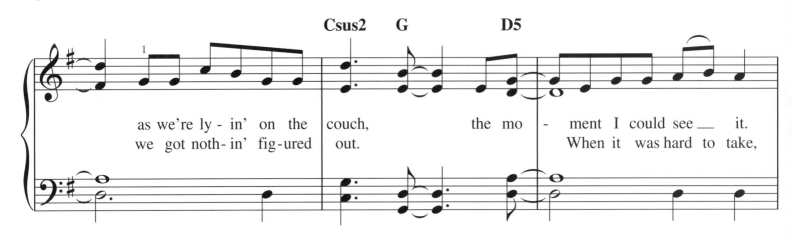

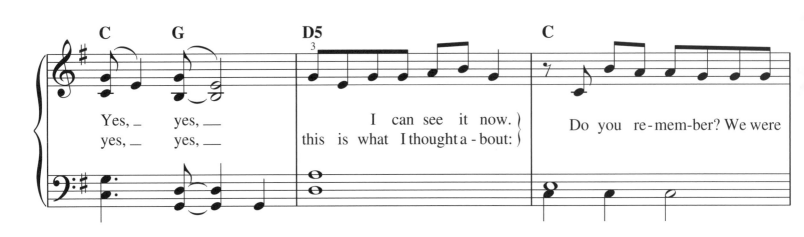

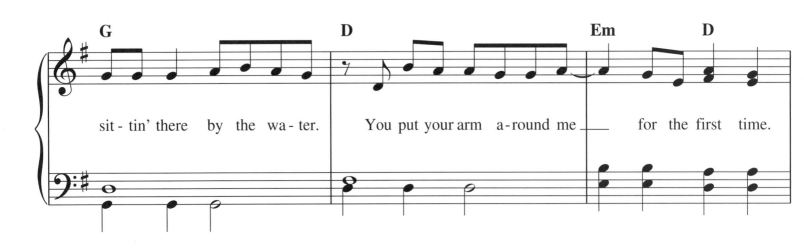

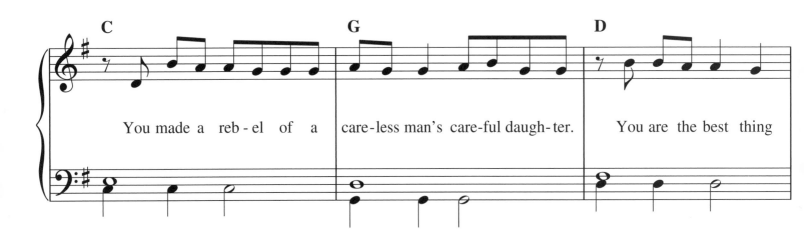

Oh, oh, ___ oh. ___

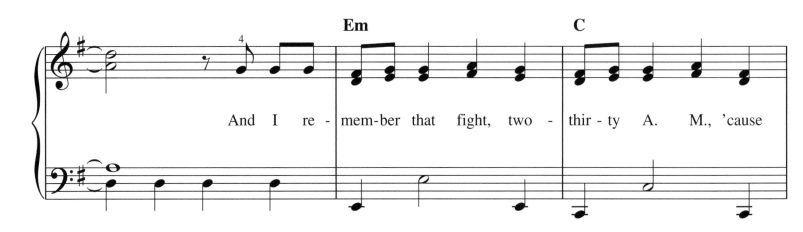

And I re - mem-ber that fight, two - thir - ty A. M., 'cause

ev -'ry-thing was slip-pin' right out of our hands. ___ I ran out cry-in' and you

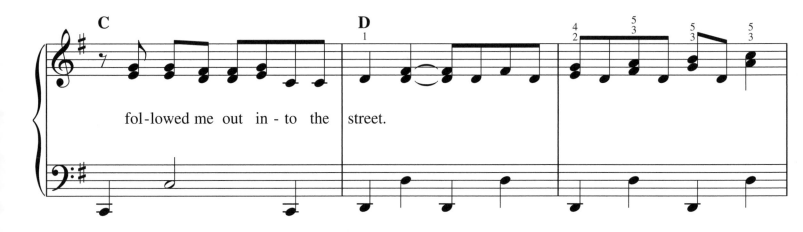

fol-lowed me out in - to the street.

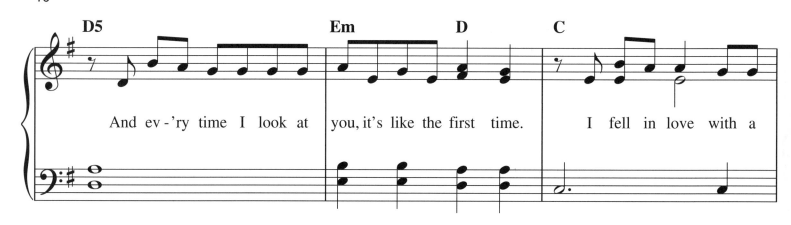

And ev-'ry time I look at you, it's like the first time. I fell in love with a

care-less man's care-ful daugh-ter. She is the best _ thing that's ev - er been _ mine."

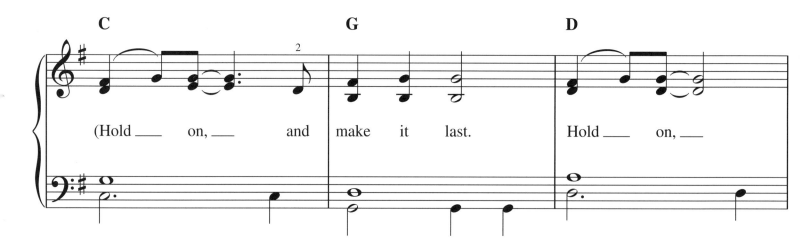

(Hold ___ on, ___ and make it last. Hold ___ on, ___

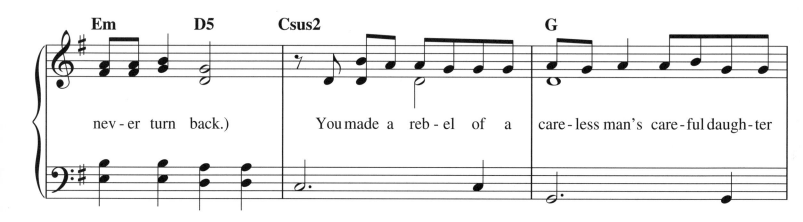

nev - er turn back.) You made a reb-el of a care-less man's care-ful daugh-ter

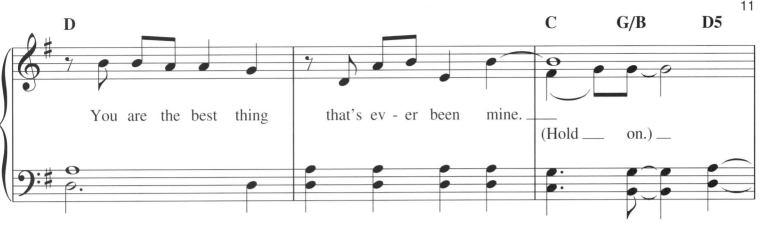
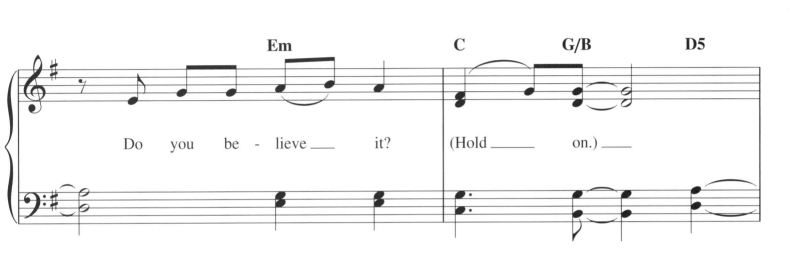
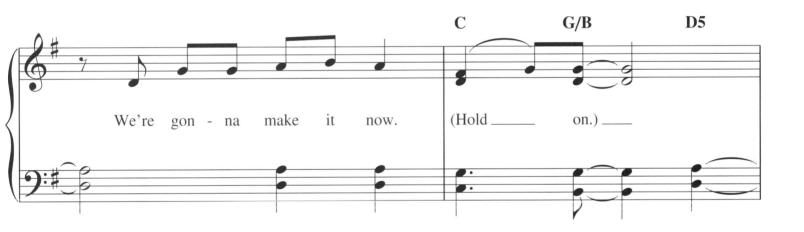
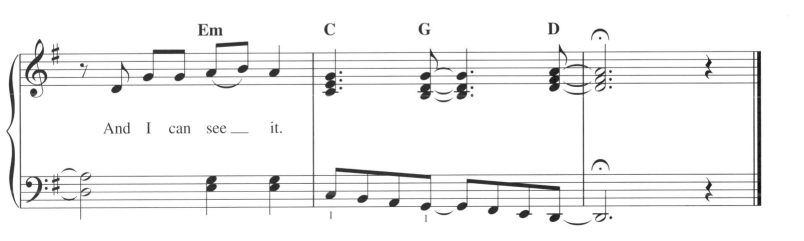

SPARKS FLY

Words and Music by
TAYLOR SWIFT

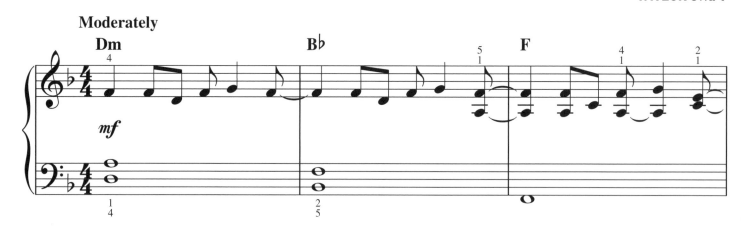

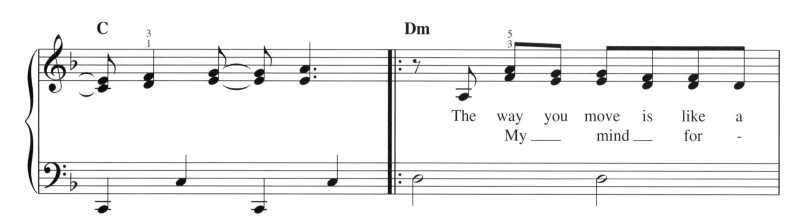

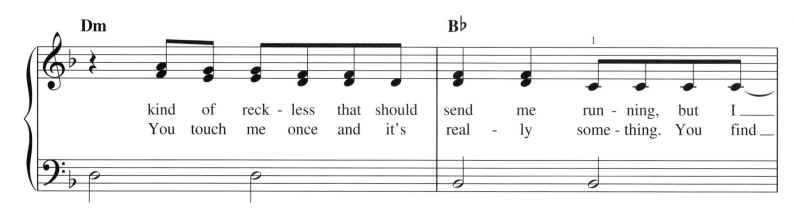

Copyright © 2010 Sony/ATV Music Publishing LLC and Taylor Swift Music
All Rights Administered by Sony/ATV Music Publishing LLC, 8 Music Square West, Nashville, TN 37203
International Copyright Secured   All Rights Reserved

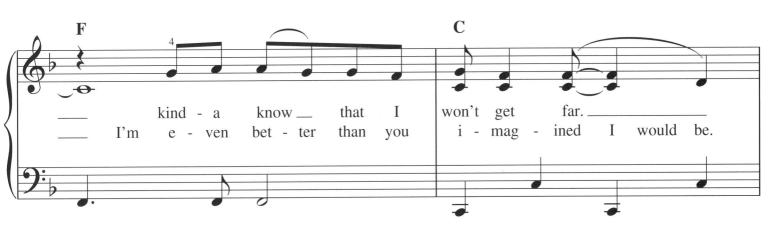

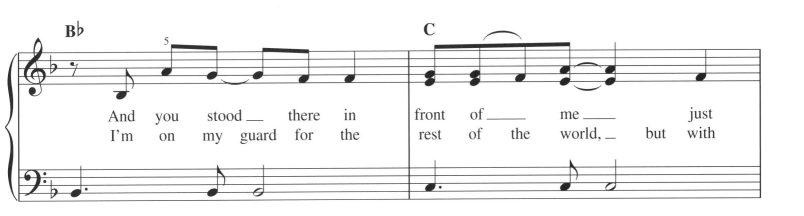

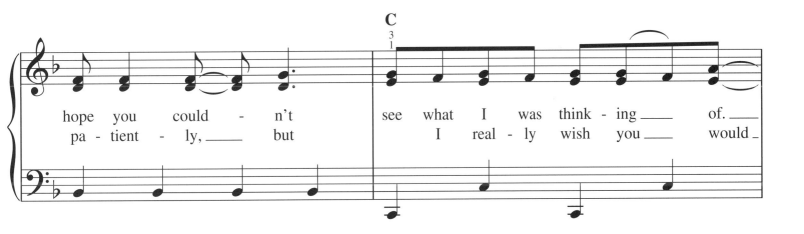

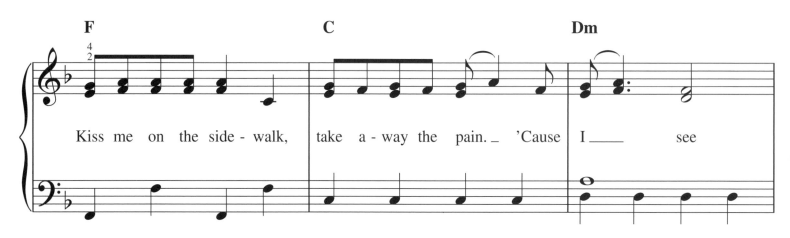

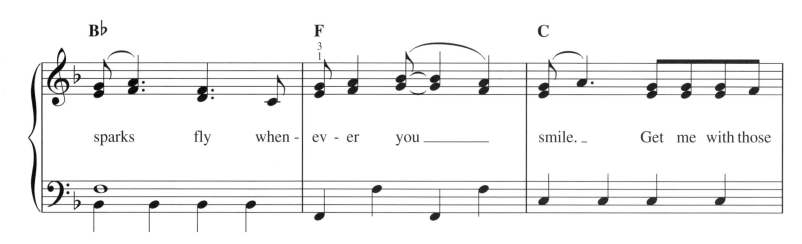

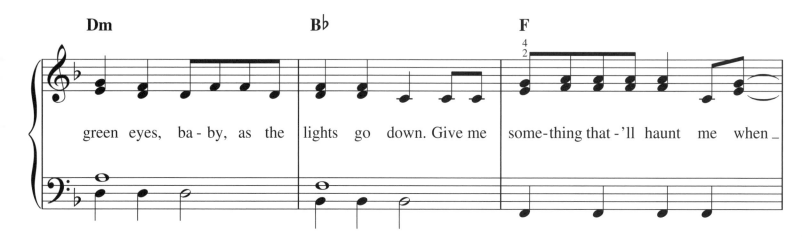

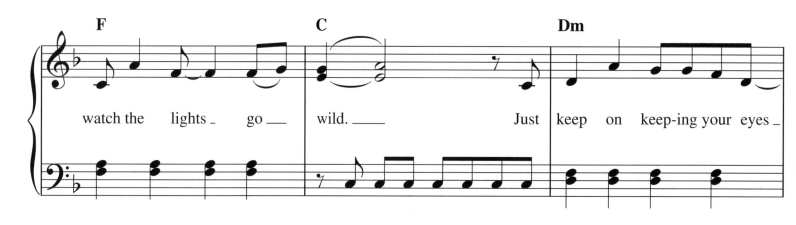

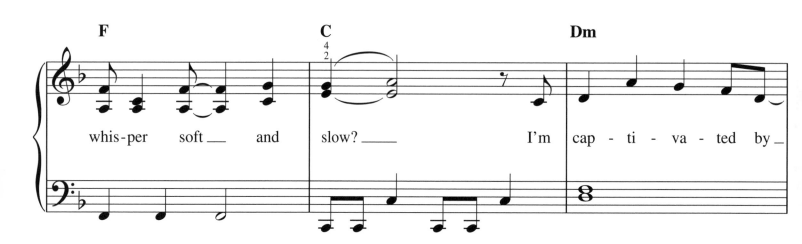

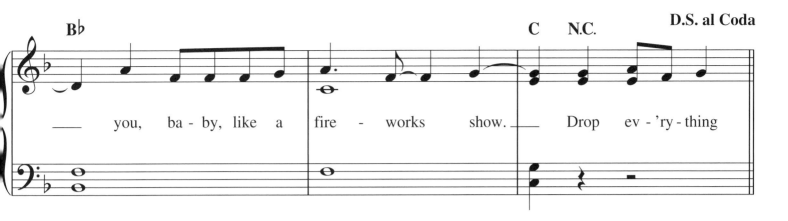

D.S. al Coda

you, ba - by, like a fire - works show.___ Drop ev - 'ry - thing

CODA

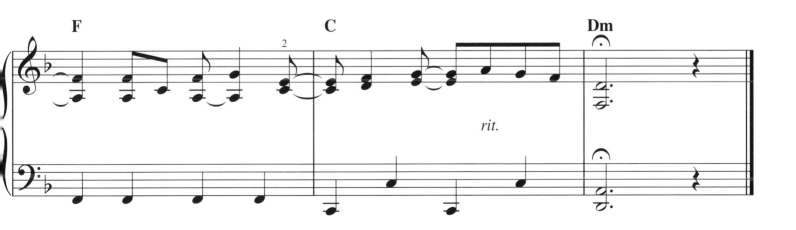

rit.

BACK TO DECEMBER

Words and Music by
TAYLOR SWIFT

1. I'm so glad you made time to see me. How's life?
2. (See additional lyrics)

Tell me, how's your fam - 'ly? I have - n't seen ____ them in ____ a

Copyright © 2010 Sony/ATV Music Publishing LLC and Taylor Swift Music
All Rights Administered by Sony/ATV Music Publishing LLC, 8 Music Square West, Nashville, TN 37203
International Copyright Secured   All Rights Reserved

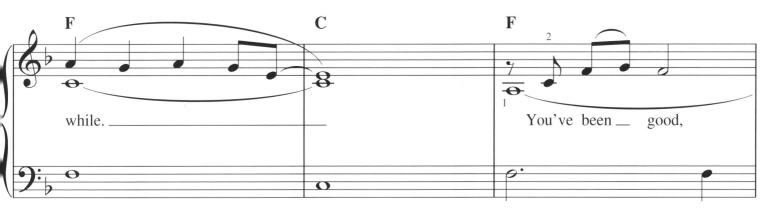

while. _____ You've been _ good,

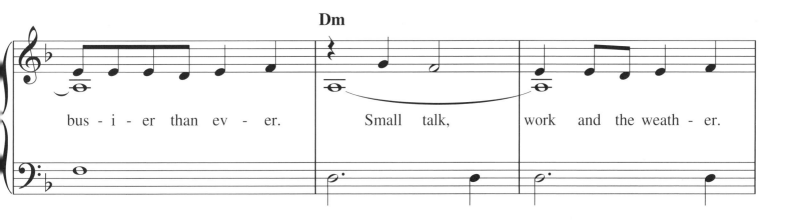

bus - i - er than ev - er. Small talk, work and the weath - er.

Your guard _ is up _ and I _ know why. _____

_ Be - cause the last time you saw me it still

burned in the back of your mind. You gave me ros - es and I ___

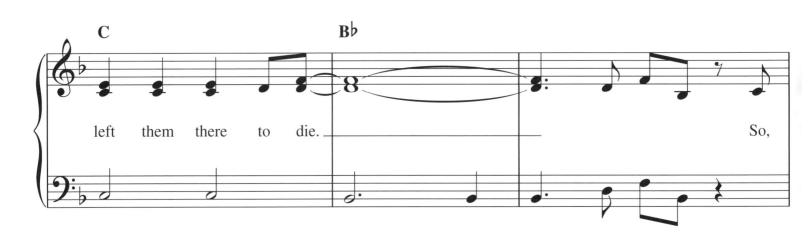

left them there to die. _____ So,

this is me swal-low-in' my pride stand-in' in front of you, say-in' I'm

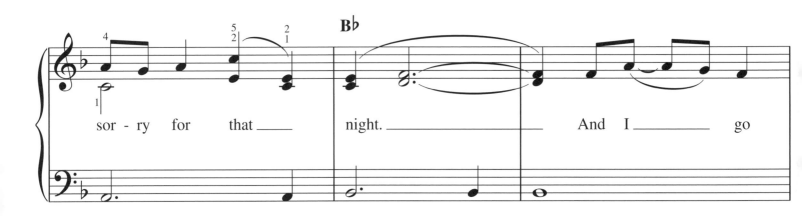

sor - ry for that ___ night. _____ And I _____ go

back to De-cem-ber all _____ the time.__ It turns out free-dom ain't

noth-in' but miss-in' you, wish-in' that I re-al-ized what I had __ when

you were mine._____ I _____ go back to De-cem-ber,

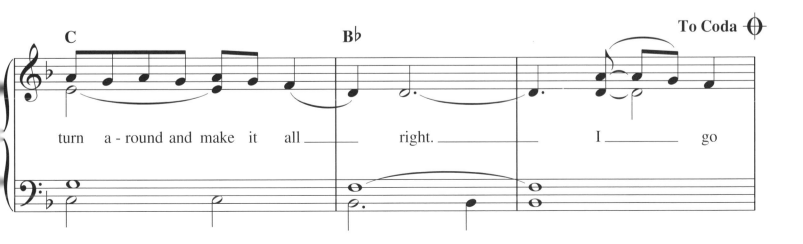

turn a-round and make it all __ right._____ I _____ go

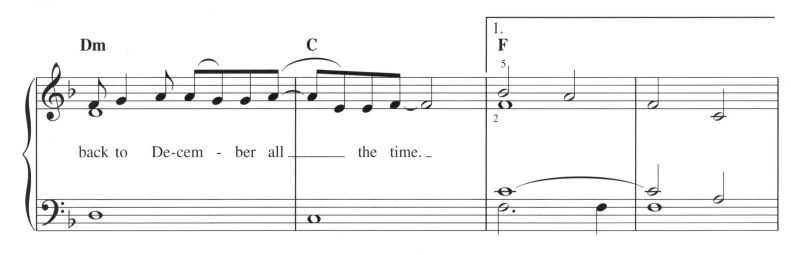

back to De-cem - ber all ____ the time. _

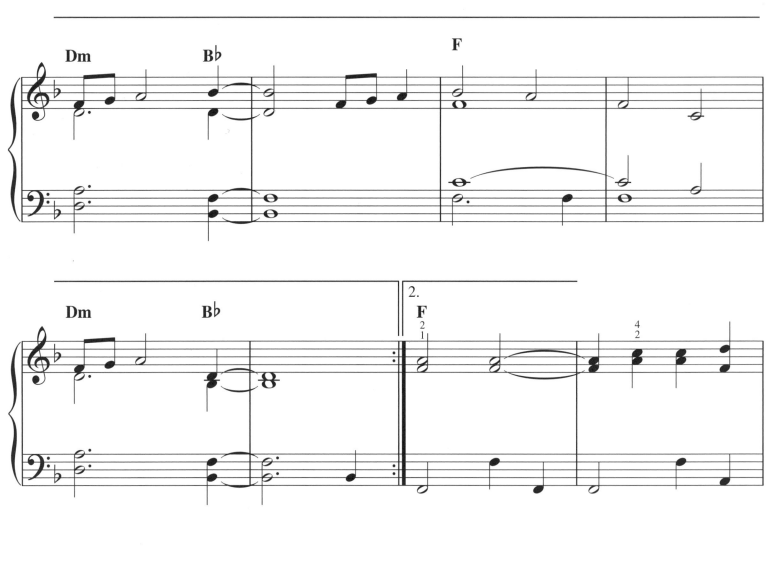

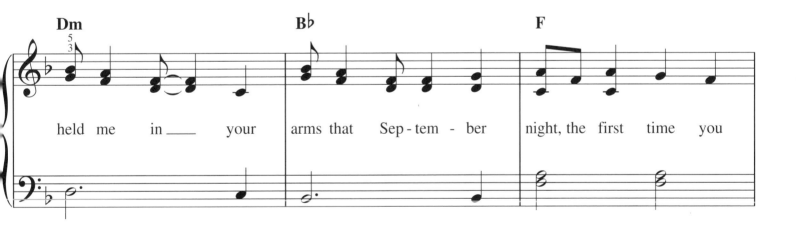

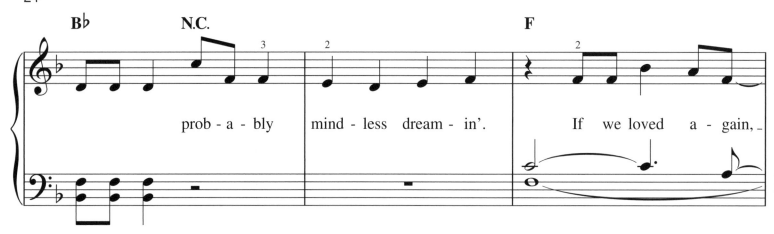

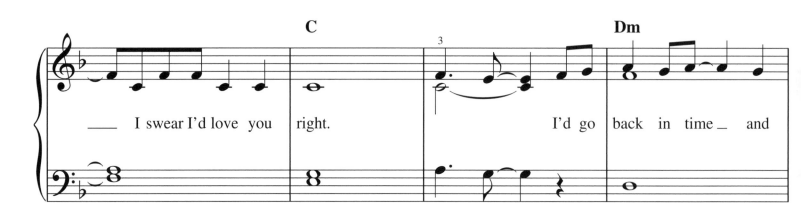

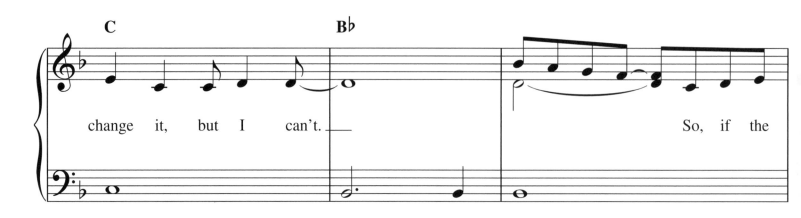

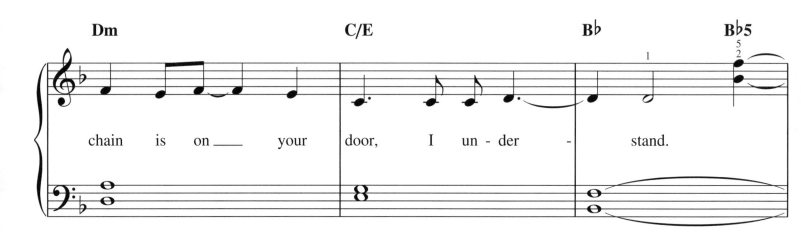

back to   De cem - ber all ____ the time. _

Additional Lyrics

2. These days I haven't been sleepin';
    Stayin' up, playin' back myself leavin',
    When your birthday passed and I didn't call.
    Then I think about summer, all the beautiful times
    I watched you laughin' from the passenger side
    And realized I loved you in the fall.
    And then the cold came, the dark days
    When fear crept into my mind.
    You gave me all your love and
    All I gave you was goodbye.

    So, this is me swallowin' my pride...

SPEAK NOW

Words and Music by
TAYLOR SWIFT

Copyright © 2010 Sony/ATV Music Publishing LLC and Taylor Swift Music
All Rights Administered by Sony/ATV Music Publishing LLC, 8 Music Square West, Nashville, TN 37203
International Copyright Secured   All Rights Reserved

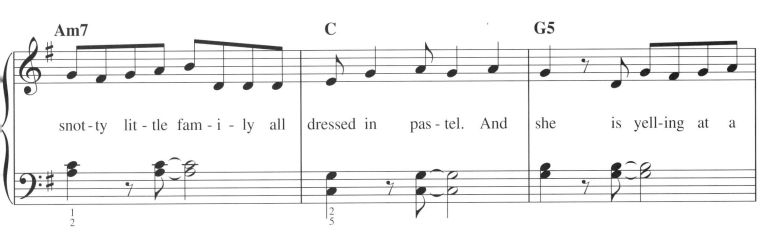

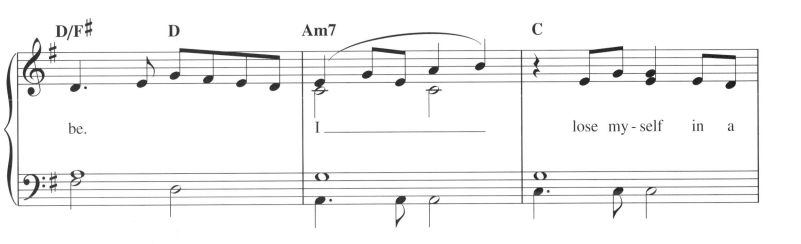

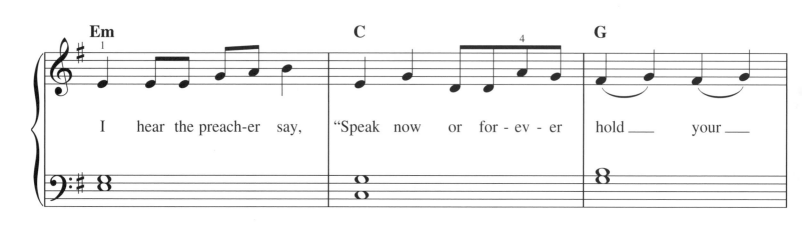

I hear the preach-er say, "Speak now or for-ev-er hold ___ your ___

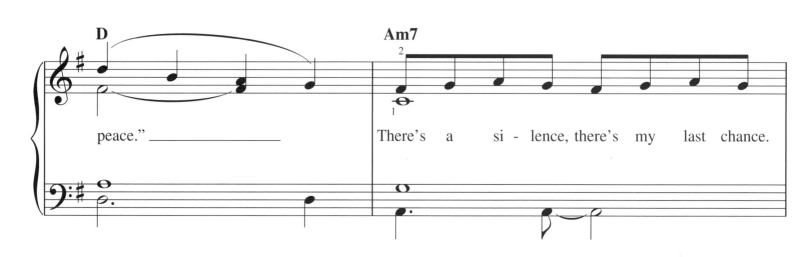

peace." ___ There's a si-lence, there's my last chance.

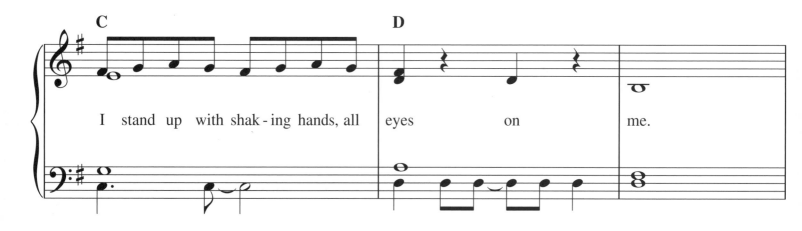

I stand up with shak-ing hands, all eyes on me.

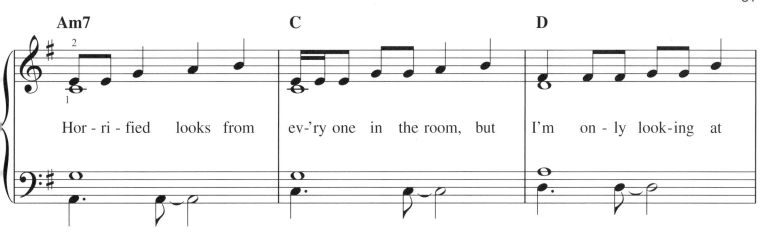

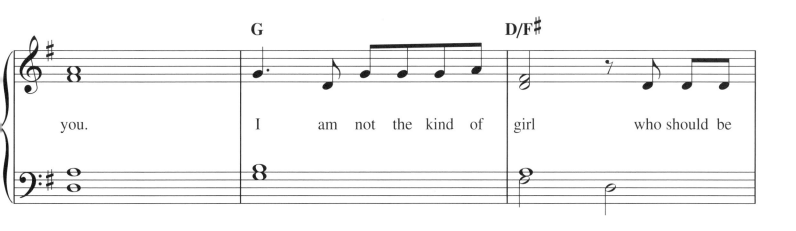

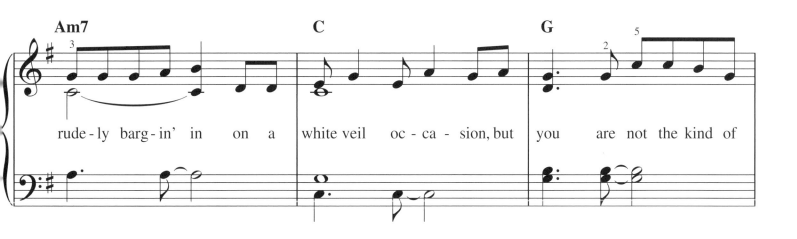

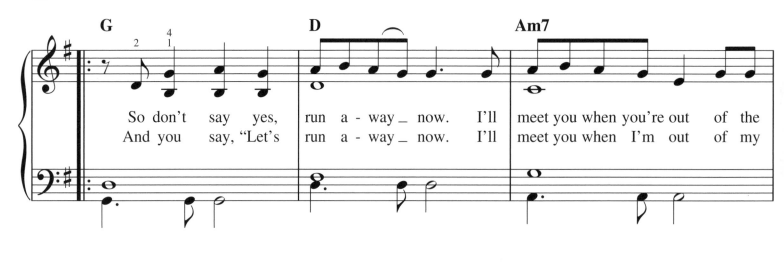

So don't say yes, run a - way _ now. I'll meet you when you're out of the
And you say, "Let's run a - way _ now. I'll meet you when I'm out of my

church at the back door. Don't wait or say a sin - gle vow. You
tux at the back door. Ba - by, I did - n't say my vows. So

need to hear me out, and they said speak now. _
glad you were a-round when they

said speak now." _

Additional Lyrics

2. Fond gestures are exchanged
   And the organ starts to play a song
   That sounds like a death march.
   And I am hiding in the curtains.
   It seems that I was uninvited by your
   Lovely bride-to-be.
   She floats down the aisle
   Like a pageant queen.
   But I know you wish it was me.
   You wish it was me, don't you?

   Don't say yes, run away now...

DEAR JOHN

Words and Music by
TAYLOR SWIFT

Moderately

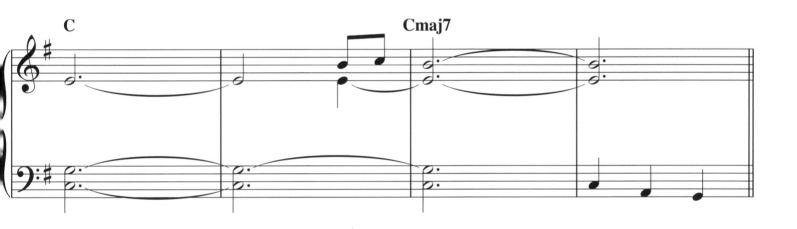

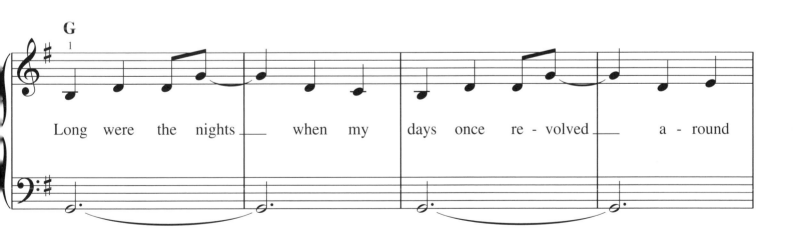

Long were the nights _____ when my days once re - volved _____ a - round

Copyright © 2010 Sony/ATV Music Publishing LLC and Taylor Swift Music
All Rights Administered by Sony/ATV Music Publishing LLC, 8 Music Square West, Nashville, TN 37203
International Copyright Secured   All Rights Reserved

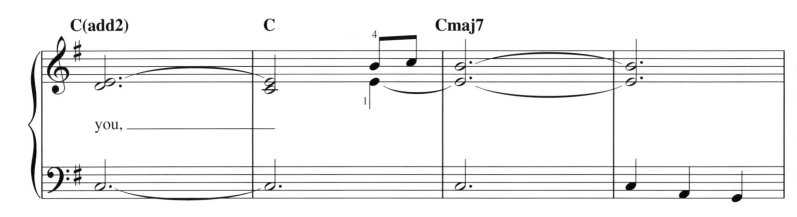

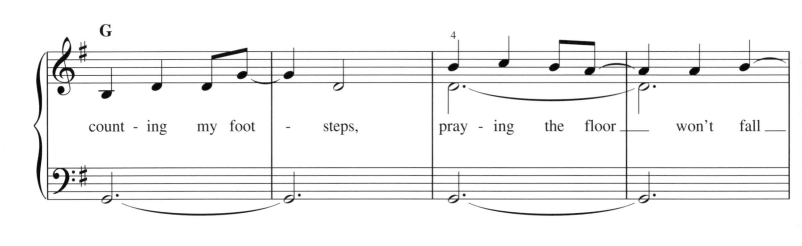

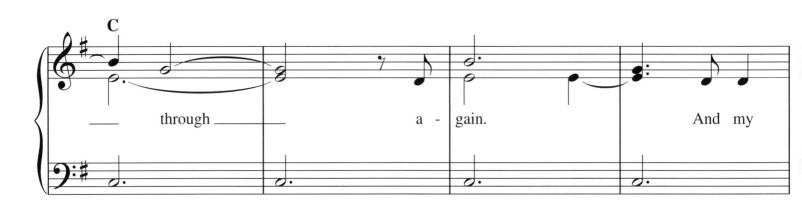

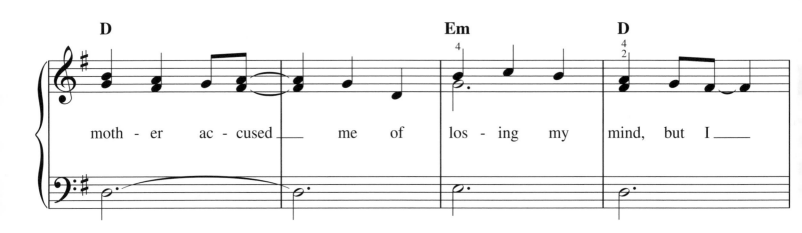

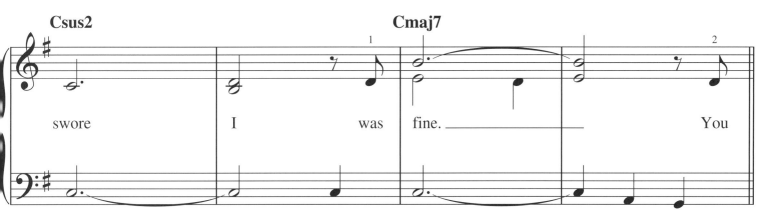

Csus2 ... Cmaj7

swore I was fine. You

G

paint me a blue sky and go back and turn it to
may - be it's me and my blind op - ti - mi - sm to

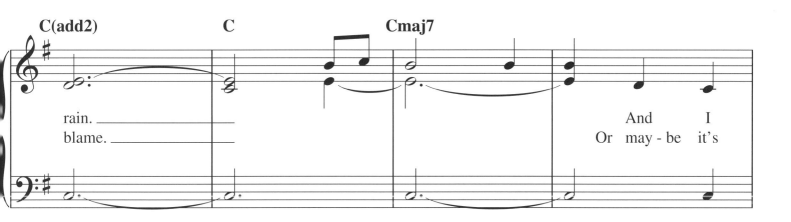

C(add2) C Cmaj7

rain. And I
blame. Or may - be it's

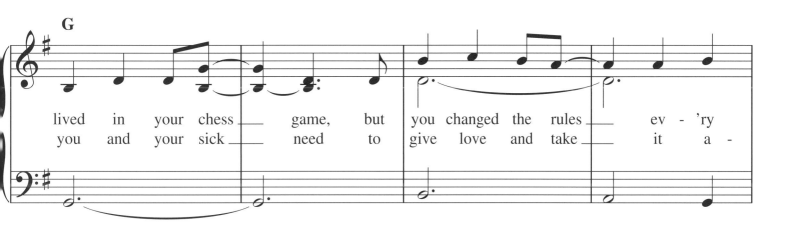

G

lived in your chess game, but you changed the rules ev - 'ry
you and your sick need to give love and take it a -

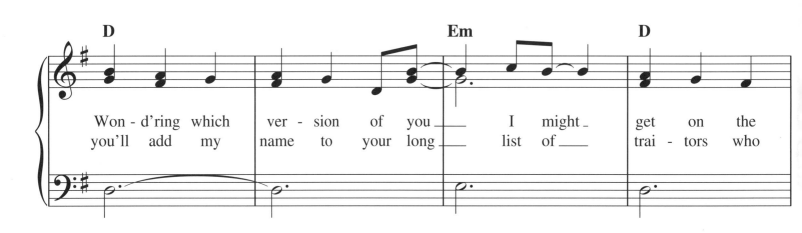

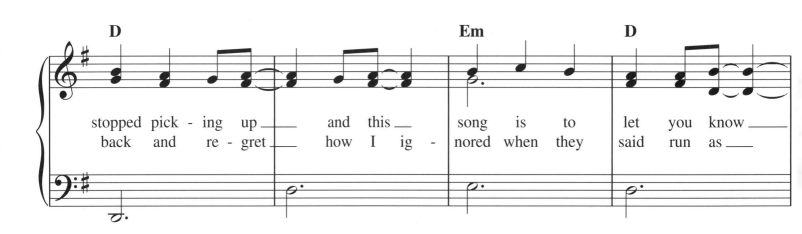

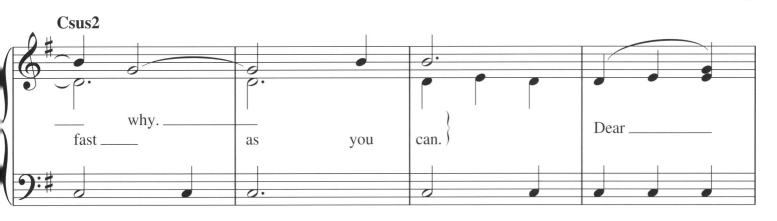

Csus2

fast why. as you can. Dear

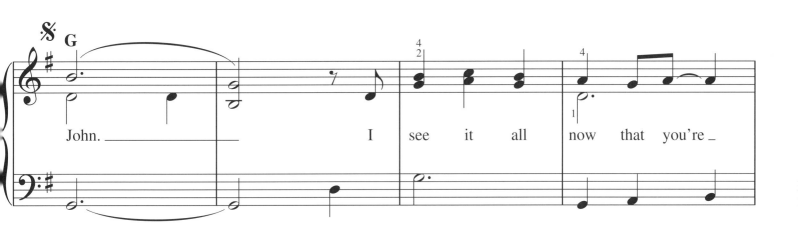

G

John. I see it all now that you're

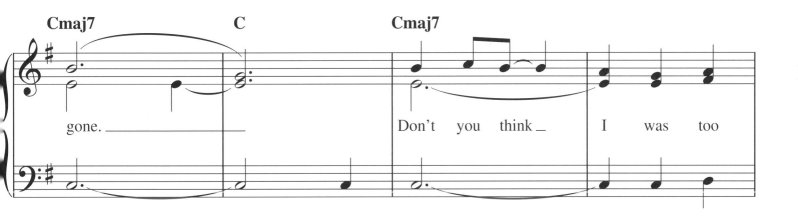

Cmaj7 **C** **Cmaj7**

gone. Don't you think I was too

Em **G/D**

young to be messed with? The girl in the dress cried the

see it all now; it was ___ wrong. ___

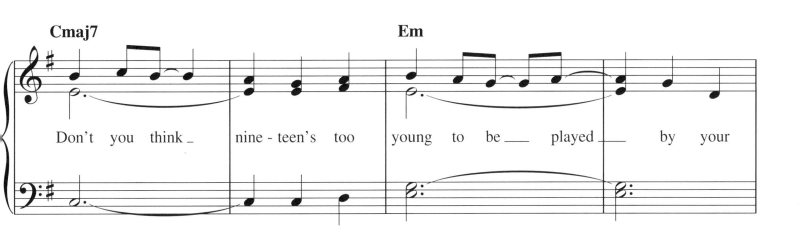

Don't you think ___ nine - teen's too young to be ___ played ___ by your

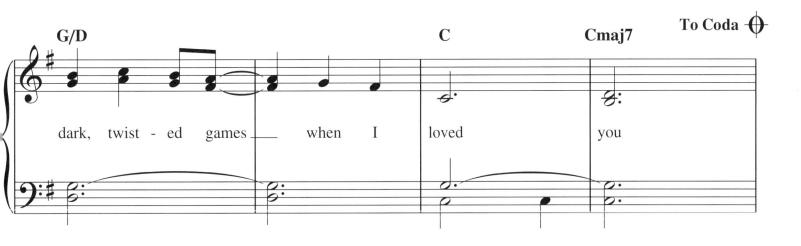

To Coda ⊕

dark, twist - ed games ___ when I loved you

so? ___ I should-'ve known ___

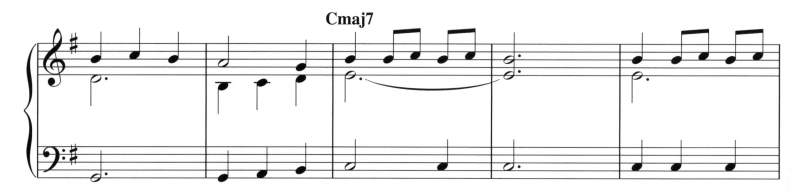

Cmaj7

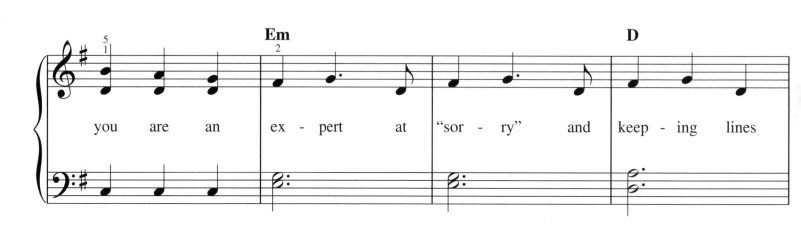

Em   **D**

you are an ex - pert at "sor - ry" and keep - ing lines

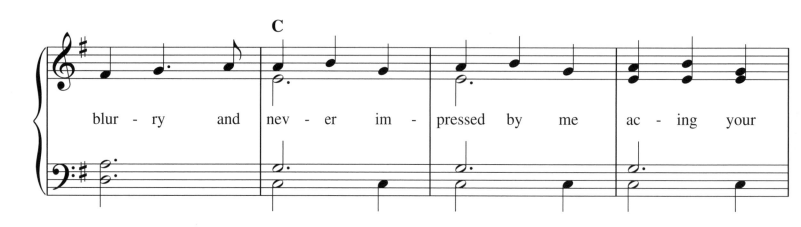

C

blur - ry and nev - er im - pressed by me ac - ing your

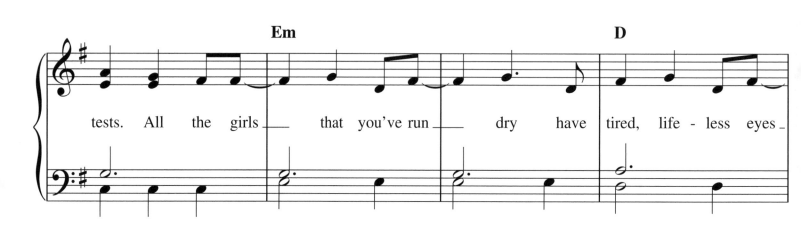

Em   **D**

tests. All the girls that you've run dry have tired, life - less eyes

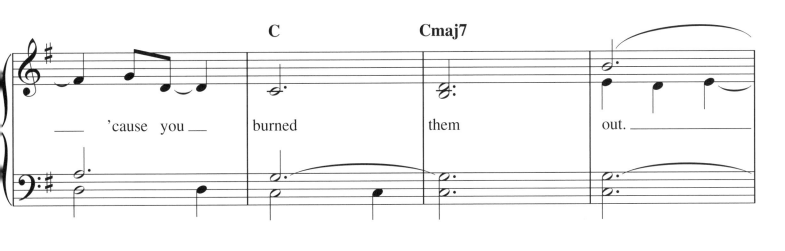

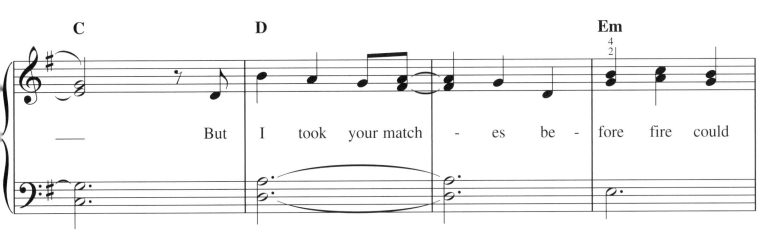

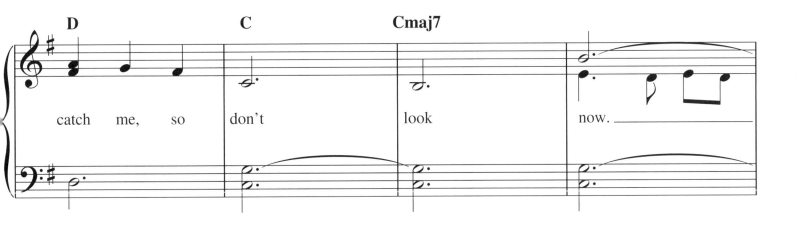

sad emp - ty town. _____

D.S. al Coda

Dear _____

CODA

so? _____ You should-'ve known.

Don't you think I was too young?

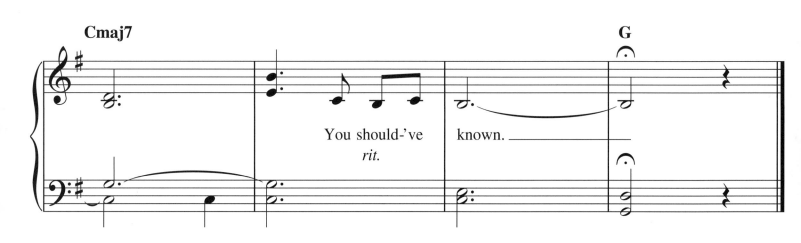

You should-'ve known. _____
rit.

MEAN

Words and Music by
TAYLOR SWIFT

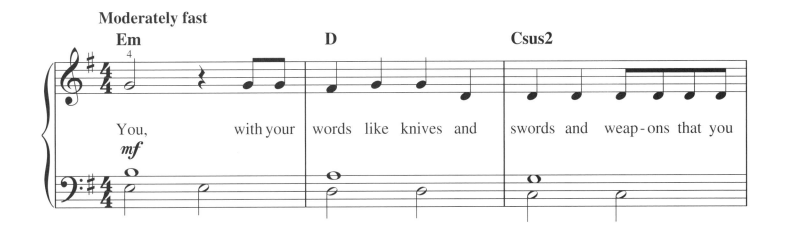

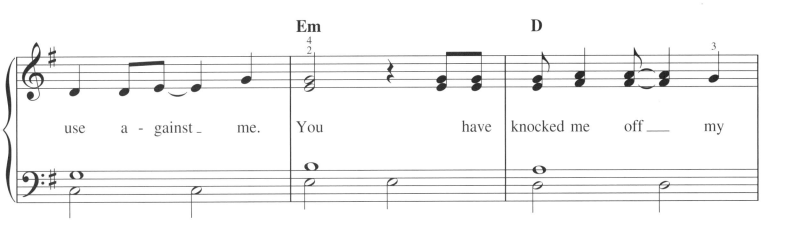

Copyright © 2010 Sony/ATV Music Publishing LLC and Taylor Swift Music
All Rights Administered by Sony/ATV Music Publishing LLC, 8 Music Square West, Nashville, TN 37203
International Copyright Secured   All Rights Reserved

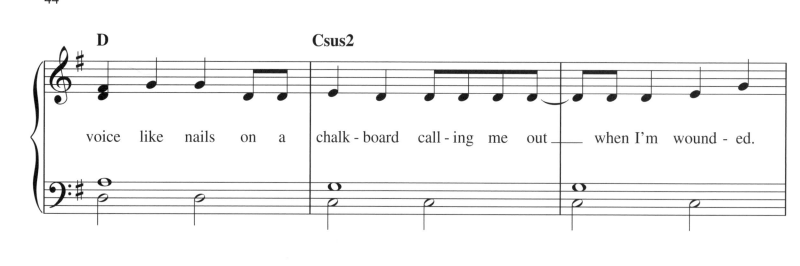

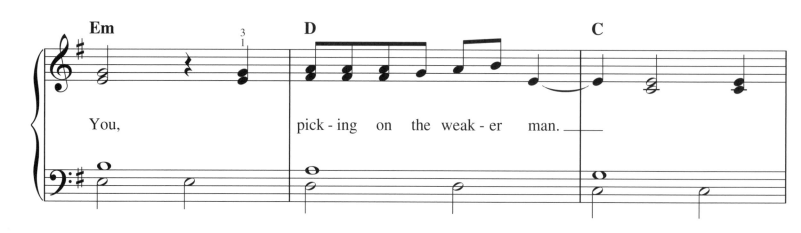

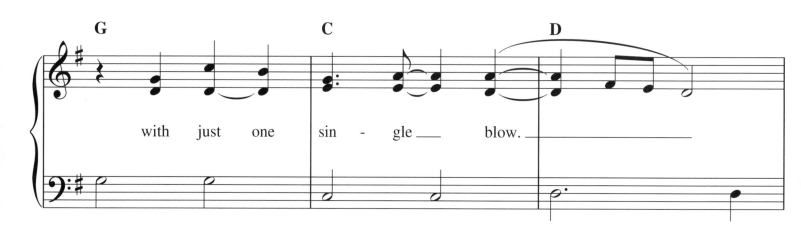

Csus2

But you don't know ___ what you don't know. ___

G　　　　**D/F♯**　　　　**Em**

Some - day ___ I'll be ___ liv - ing in a big ole

C　　　　**G**　　　　**D**

cit - y, ___ and all you're ___ ev - er gon - na be is

C　　　　　　　　**G**

mean. Some - day ___

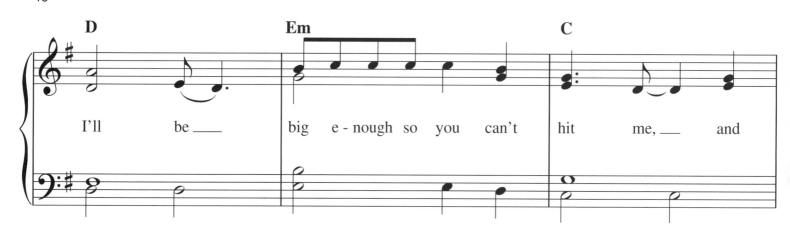

I'll   be ____   big e - nough so you can't   hit   me, ____   and

all   you're   ev - er gon - na be   is   mean.

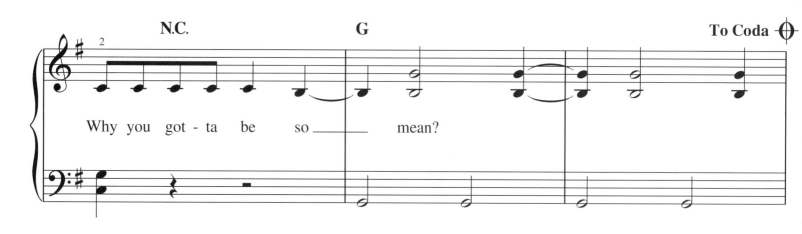

Why you got - ta   be   so ____   mean?

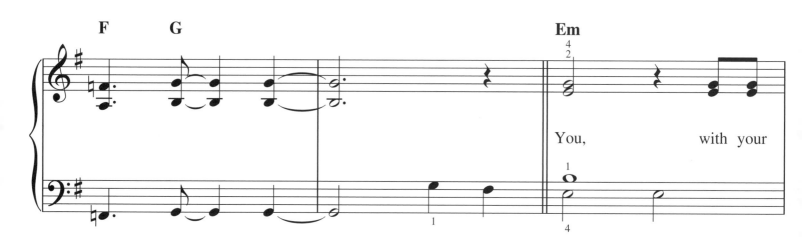

You,   with your

switch - ing   sides   and your   wild - fire   lies   and your   hu - mil - i - a - tion.

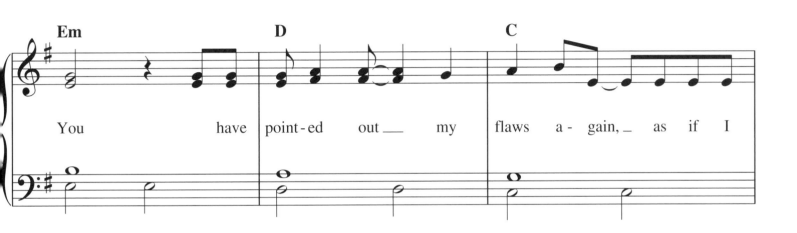

You   have   point - ed   out __   my   flaws   a - gain, __   as   if   I

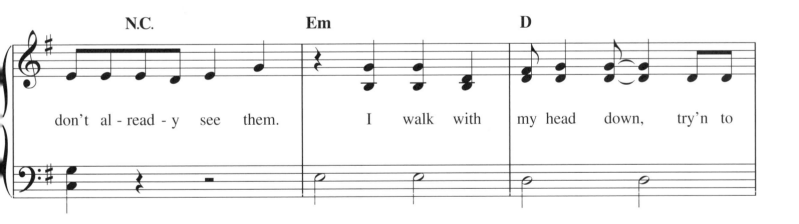

don't   al - read - y   see   them.   I   walk   with   my   head   down,   try'n   to

block   you   out 'cause I'll   nev - er   im - press   you.   I   just

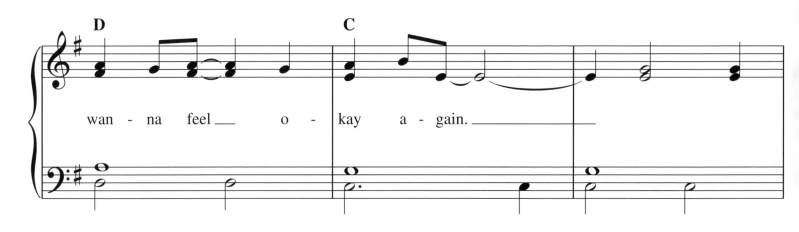

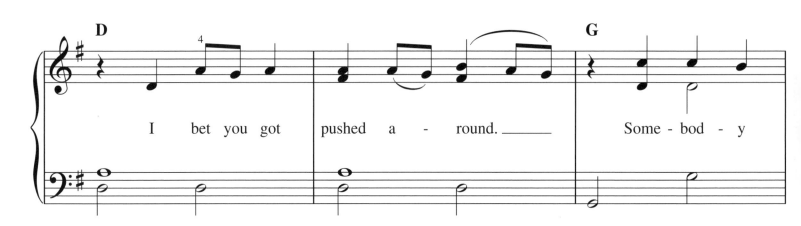

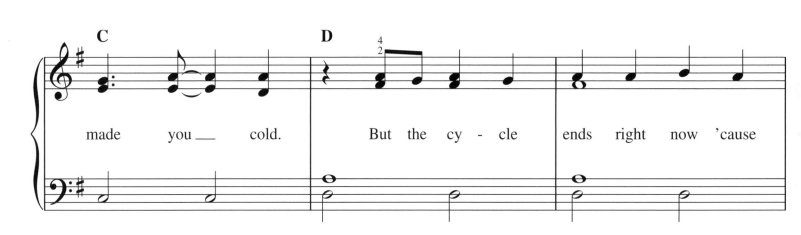

D.S. al Coda

CODA

F   G

you don't know. ___

And I ___ can | see you years ___ from | now in a bar,

talk - ing o - ver a | foot - ball ___ game | with that same big,

loud o - pin - ion, but | no - bod - y's | lis - ten - ing.

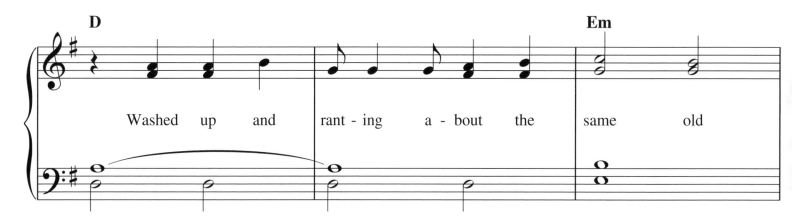

Washed up and rant - ing a - bout the same old

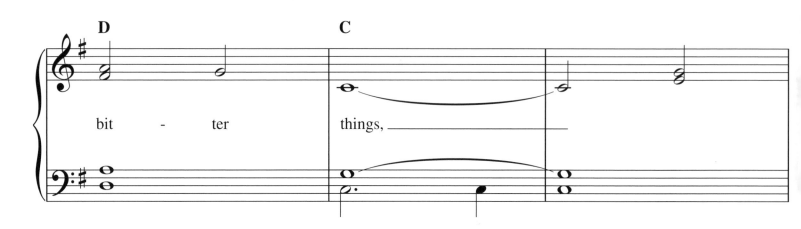

bit - ter things, _____

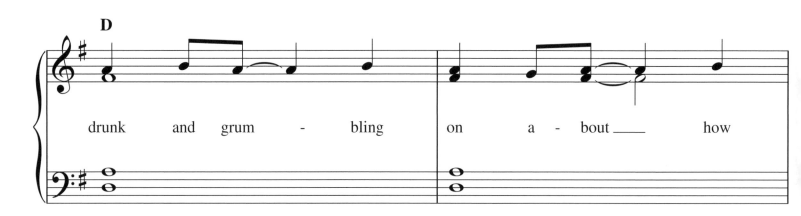

drunk and grum - bling on a - bout _____ how

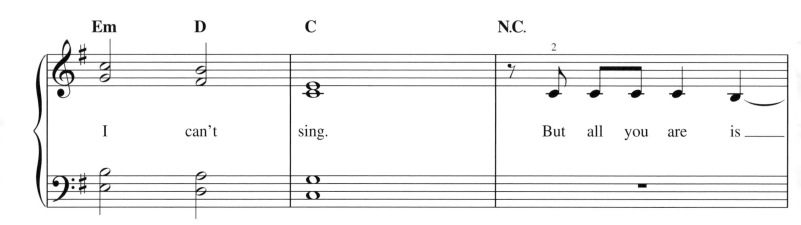

I can't sing. But all you are is _____

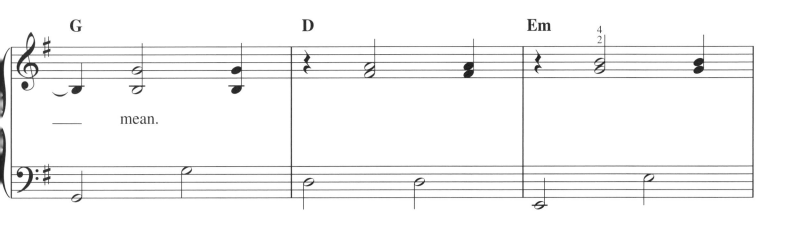

G   **D**   **Em**

_____ mean.

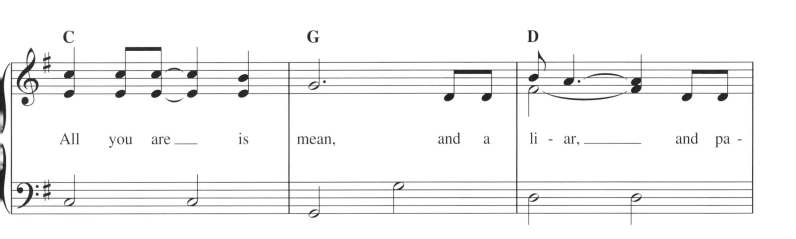

C   **G**   **D**

All you are ___ is mean, and a li - ar, _____ and pa -

Em   **C**   **G**

thet - ic, _____ and a - lone in life, ___ and mean and

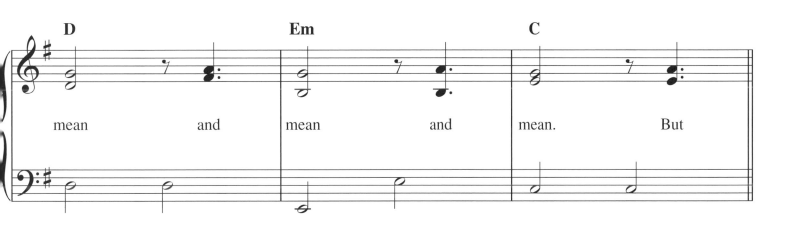

D   **Em**   **C**

mean and mean and mean. But

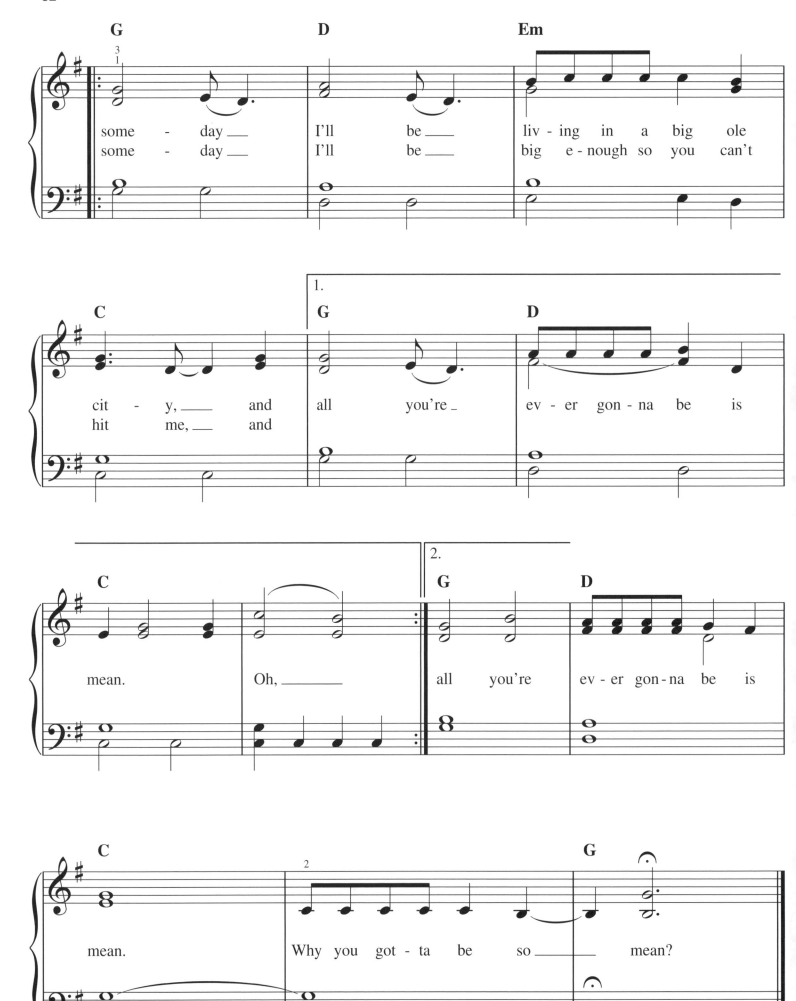

THE STORY OF US

Words and Music by
TAYLOR SWIFT

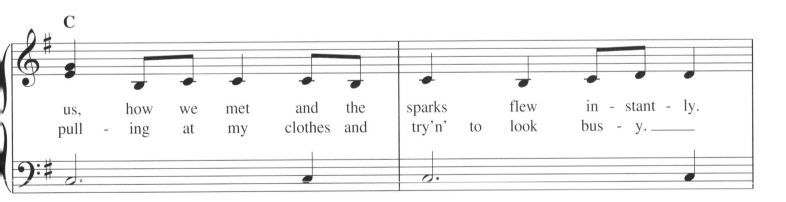

Copyright © 2010 Sony/ATV Music Publishing LLC and Taylor Swift Music
All Rights Administered by Sony/ATV Music Publishing LLC, 8 Music Square West, Nashville, TN 37203
International Copyright Secured   All Rights Reserved

54

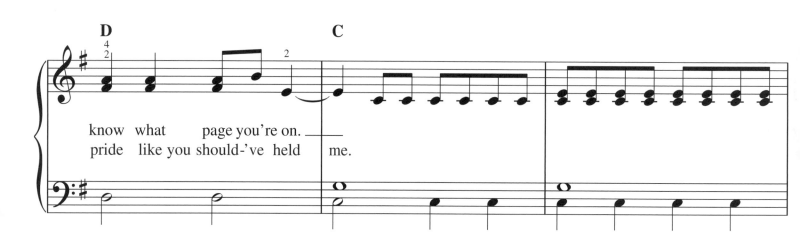

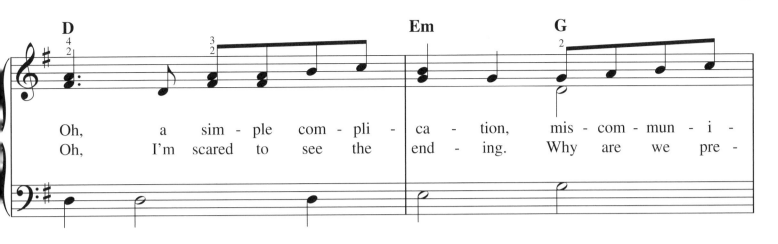

Oh, a sim - ple com - pli - ca - tion, mis - com - mun - i -
Oh, I'm scared to see the end - ing. Why are we pre -

ca - tions lead to fall - out. So man - y things _ that I
tend - ing this is noth - ing? I'd tell you I miss _ you but I

wish you knew, _ so man - y walls _ up, I can't break through. _ }
don't know how. _ I nev - er heard _ si - lence quite this loud. _ }

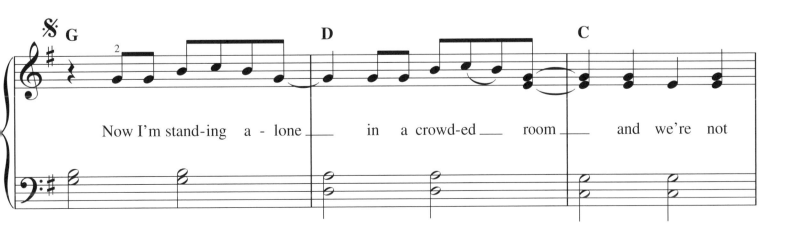

Now I'm stand - ing a - lone _ in a crowd - ed _ room _ and we're not

speak - ing. ___ And I'm dy - ing to know, ___ is it kill - ing ___ you ___

___ like it's kill - ing me? ___ Yeah. I don't know what to

say since the twist of fate, when it all broke down. And the

To Coda

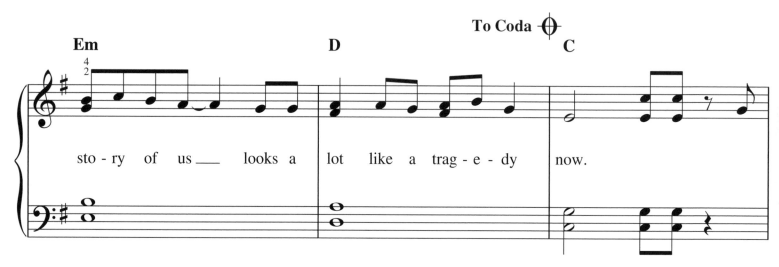

sto - ry of us ___ looks a lot like a trag - e - dy now.

Next chap - ter.

This is look - ing like a   con - test

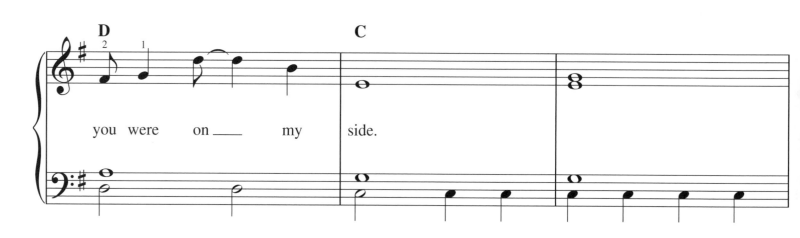

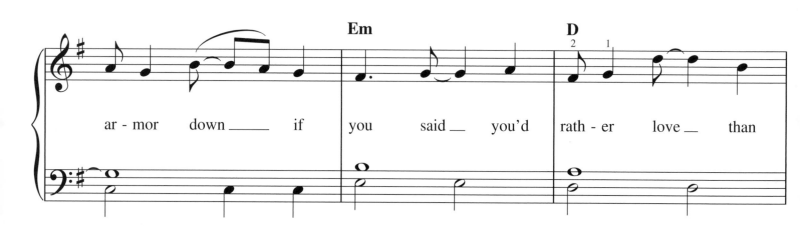

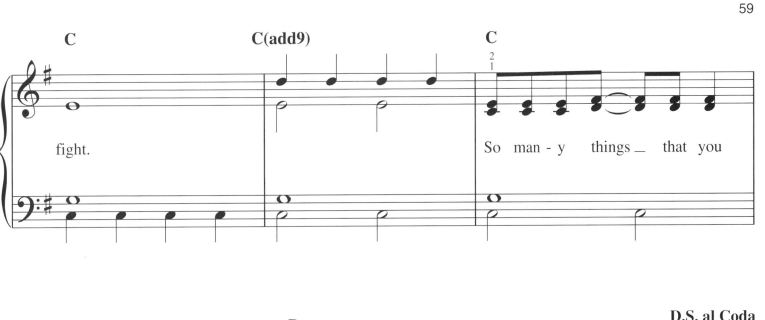

NEVER GROW UP

Words and Music by
TAYLOR SWIFT

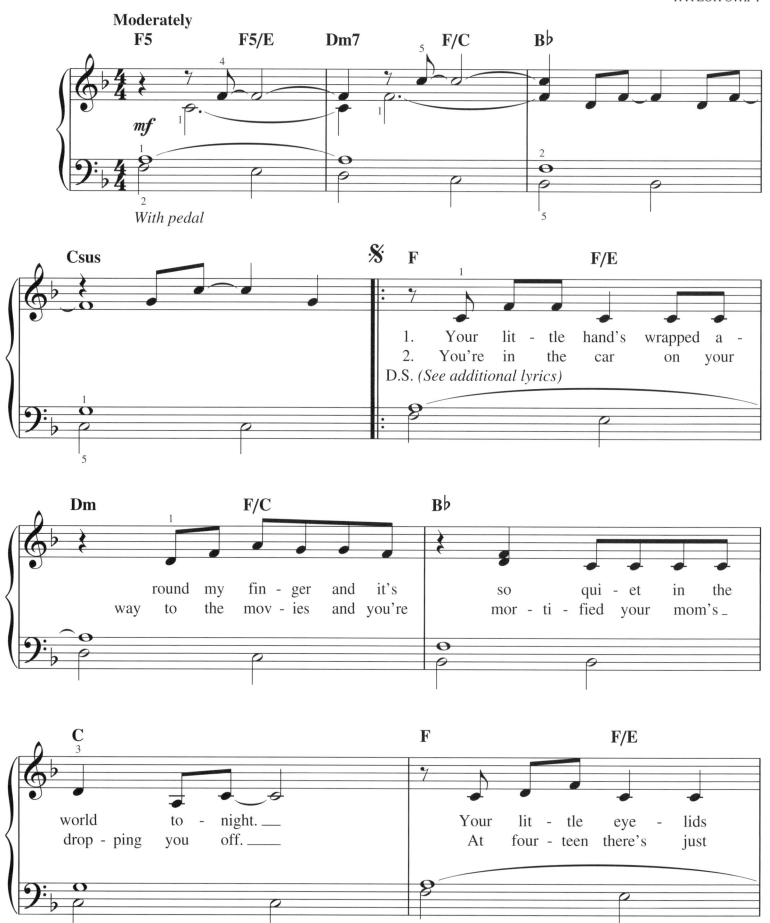

1. Your lit - tle hand's wrapped a -
2. You're in the car on your

D.S. (See additional lyrics)

round my fin - ger and it's
way to the mov - ies and you're

so qui - et in the
mor - ti - fied your mom's

world to - night. ___
drop - ping you off. ___

Your lit - tle eye - lids
At four - teen there's just

Copyright © 2010 Sony/ATV Music Publishing LLC and Taylor Swift Music
All Rights Administered by Sony/ATV Music Publishing LLC, 8 Music Square West, Nashville, TN 37203
International Copyright Secured   All Rights Reserved

C

if you could stay like that.
in your p - j's get - ting read - y for school. Oh, dar - ling, don't you

F   **F/E**

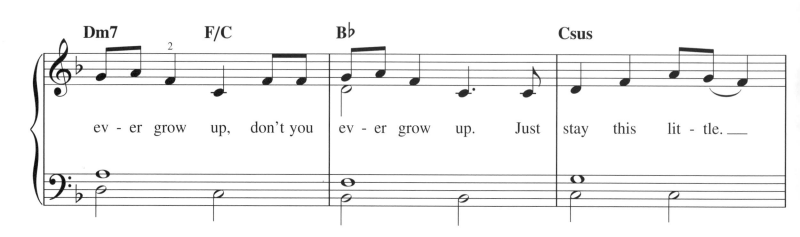

Dm7   **F/C**   **Bb**   **Csus**

ev - er grow up, don't you ev - er grow up. Just stay this lit - tle.___

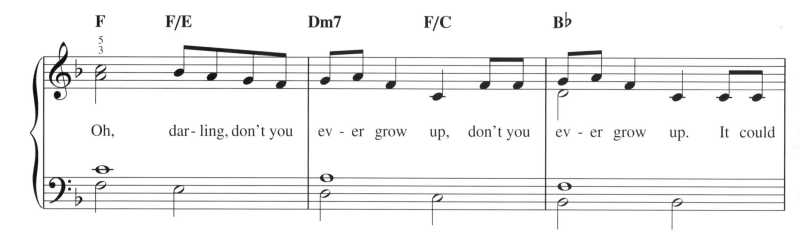

F   **F/E**   **Dm7**   **F/C**   **Bb**

Oh, dar - ling, don't you ev - er grow up, don't you ev - er grow up. It could

To Coda ⊕

Csus   **Bb**

stay this sim - ple.___ I won't let no - bod - y hurt you,
No one's ev - er burned you ___

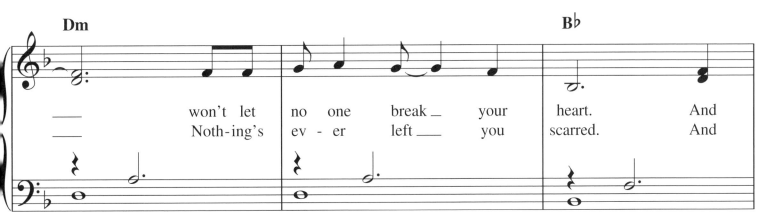

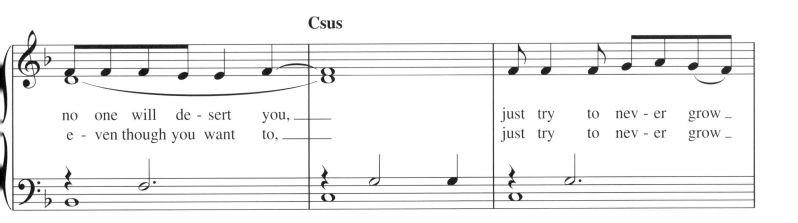

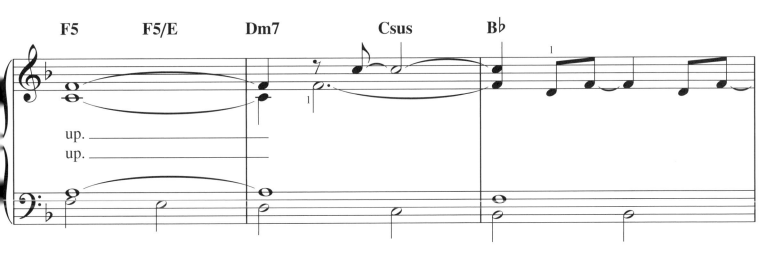

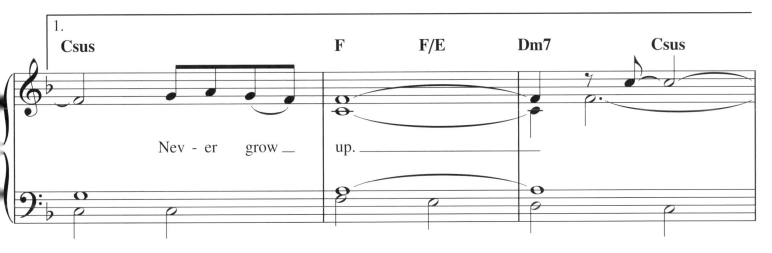

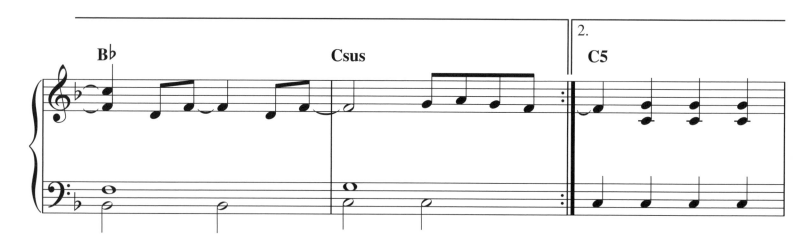

Take pic-tures in your mind of your child - hood room. _____

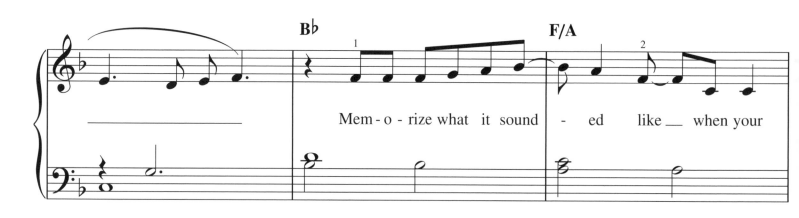

_____ Mem-o-rize what it sound - ed like __ when your

dad gets home. _____ Re-mem-ber the foot - steps, re-mem-ber the words __

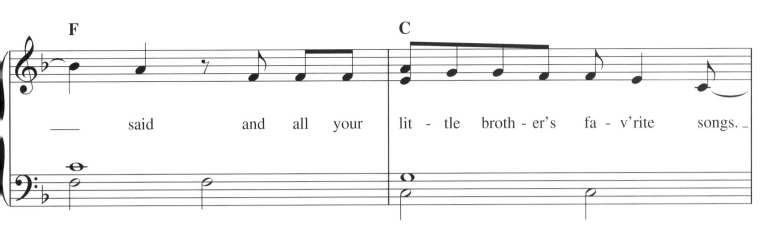

said and all your lit - tle broth - er's fa - v'rite songs. _

_ I just re - al - ized ev - 'ry - thing _ I

have is some-day gon - na be gone.

D.S. al Coda

CODA

F **F/E**

Won't let _

_ no - bod - y hurt you. _ Won't let no one break _ your

Additional Lyrics

So, here I am in my new apartment in a big city;
They just dropped me off.
It's so much colder than I thought it would be,
So I tuck myself in and turn my nightlight on.
Wish I'd never grown up.
I wish I'd never grown up.
Oh, I don't wanna grow up.
Wish I'd never grown up.
I could still be little.
Oh, I don't wanna grow up.
Wish I'd never grown up.
It could still be simple.
Oh, darling, don't you ever grow up,
Don't you ever grow up.
Just stay this little.
Oh, darling don't you ever grow up,
Don't you ever grow up.
It could stay this simple.

ENCHANTED

Words and Music by
TAYLOR SWIFT

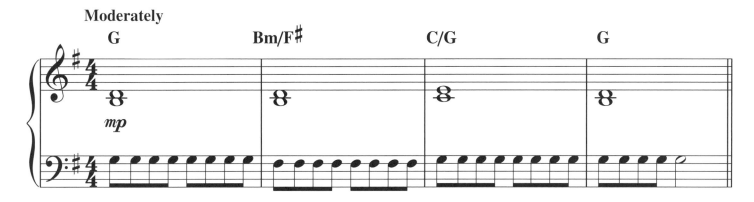

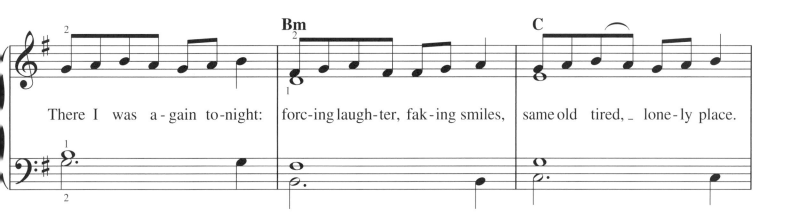

Copyright © 2010 Sony/ATV Music Publishing LLC and Taylor Swift Music
All Rights Administered by Sony/ATV Music Publishing LLC, 8 Music Square West, Nashville, TN 37203
International Copyright Secured   All Rights Reserved

struck, danc-ing a-round all a - lone. ___ I'll spend for - ev - er won-d'ring if you

knew I was en-chant-ed to meet ___ you. _____

This is me pray-ing that this was the ver - y first page, not where the sto - ry-line ends.

BETTER THAN REVENGE

Words and Music by
TAYLOR SWIFT

Copyright © 2010 Sony/ATV Music Publishing LLC and Taylor Swift Music
All Rights Administered by Sony/ATV Music Publishing LLC, 8 Music Square West, Nashville, TN 37203
International Copyright Secured   All Rights Reserved

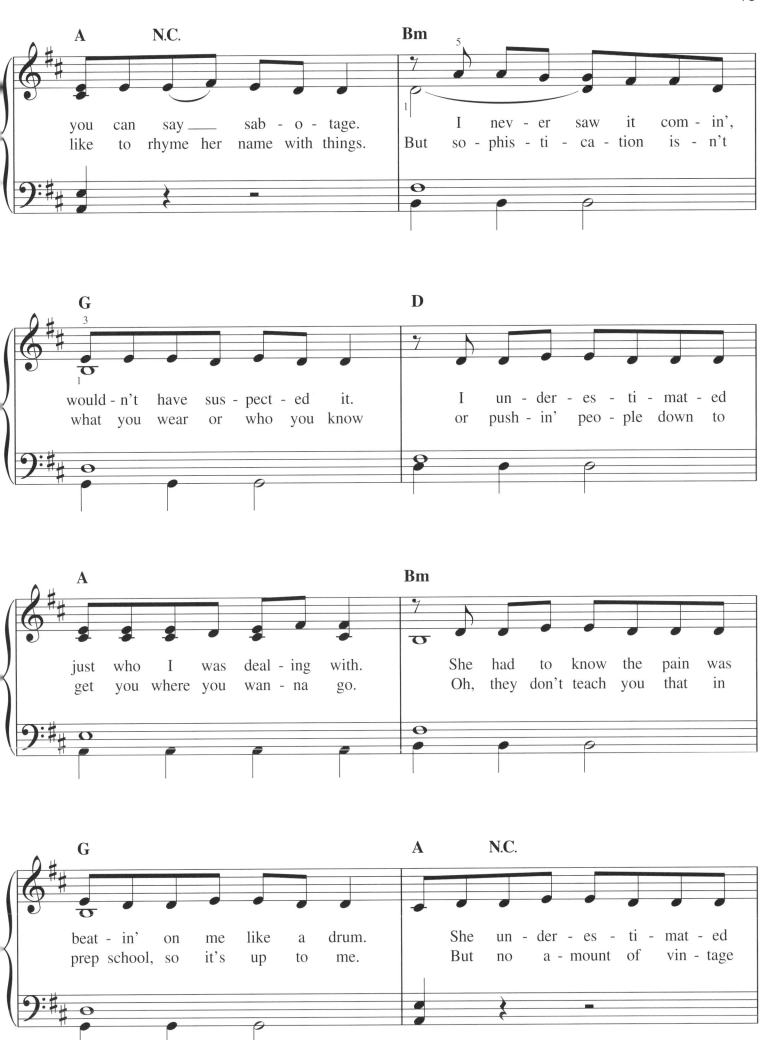

G   **Bm**   **G**

friends. _

She should keep in mind, she should | keep in mind there is noth-ing

A   **To Coda**   1.   2.   **G**

I   do   bet-ter than re - | venge.   venge.

A/C#   **Bm**

I'm | just an - oth - er thing for you to | roll your eyes at, hon - ey.   You

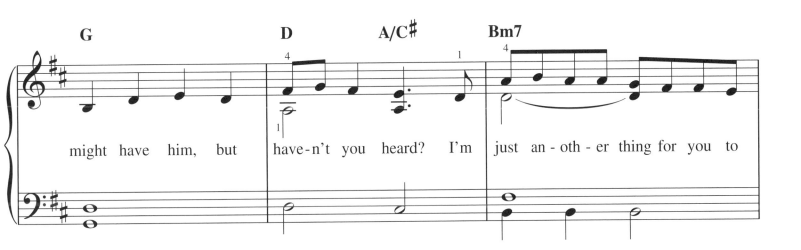

G   **D**   **A/C#**   **Bm7**

might   have   him,   but | have-n't you heard?   I'm | just an - oth - er thing for you to

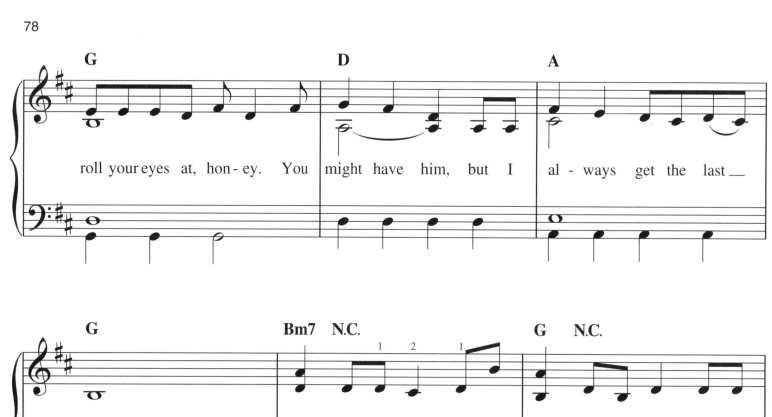

G   **D**   **A**

roll your eyes at, hon - ey. You might have him, but I al - ways get the last __

G   **Bm7 N.C.**   **G N.C.**

word.   She's not a saint and she's not what you think. She's an

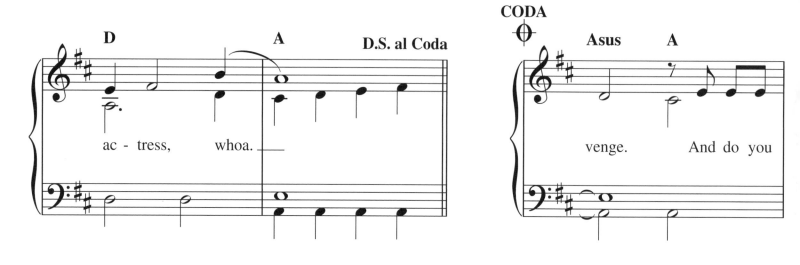

D   **A**   **D.S. al Coda**

ac - tress, whoa. __

CODA

Asus   **A**

venge.   And do you

Bm   **G**   **D**

still feel like you know what you're do - in'? 'Cause I don't think you

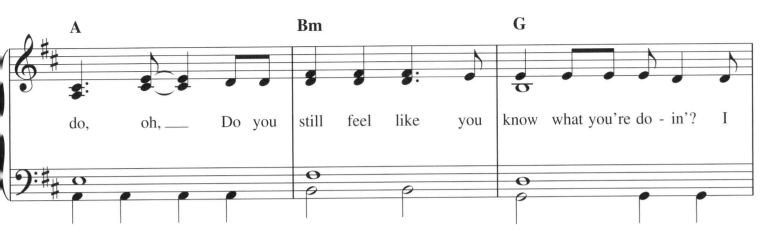

do, oh, ___ Do you still feel like you know what you're do - in'? I

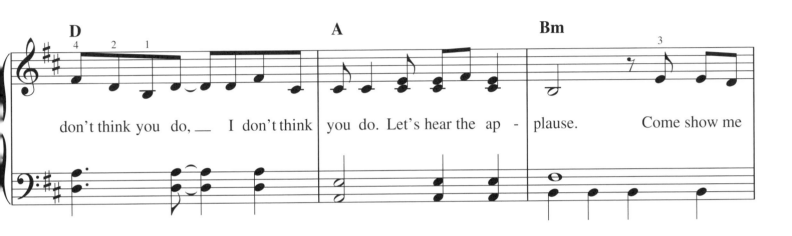

don't think you do, ___ I don't think you do. Let's hear the ap - plause. Come show me

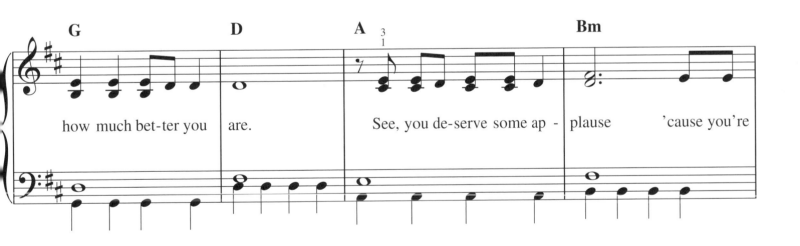

how much bet-ter you are. See, you de-serve some ap - plause 'cause you're

so much bet - ter. She took him fast - er than you can say sab - o - tage.

INNOCENT

Words and Music by
TAYLOR SWIFT

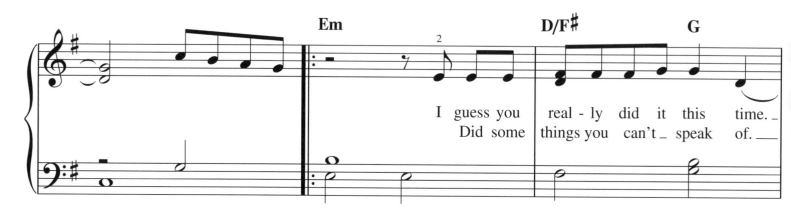

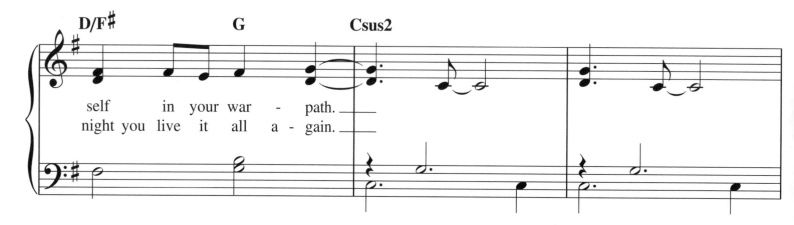

Copyright © 2010 Sony/ATV Music Publishing LLC and Taylor Swift Music
All Rights Administered by Sony/ATV Music Publishing LLC, 8 Music Square West, Nashville, TN 37203
International Copyright Secured   All Rights Reserved

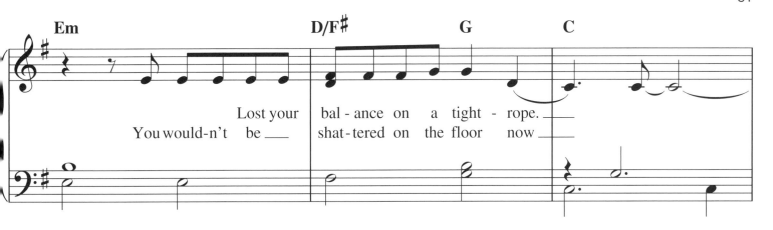

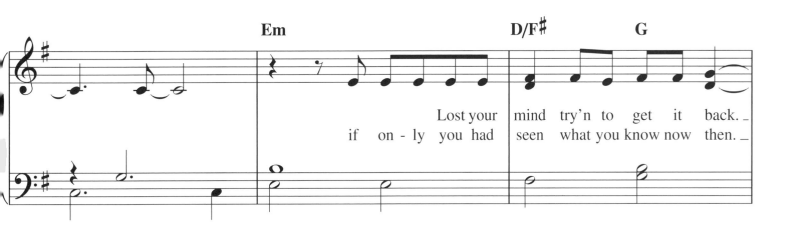

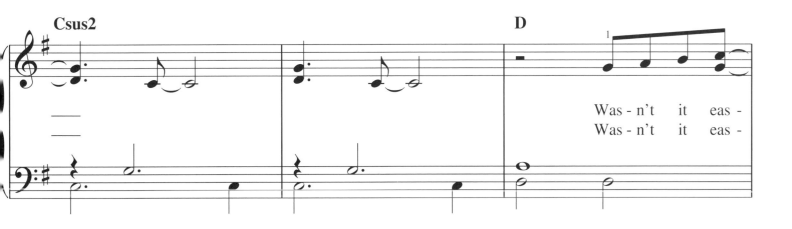

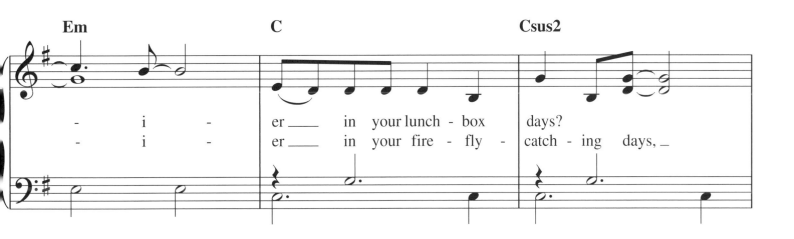

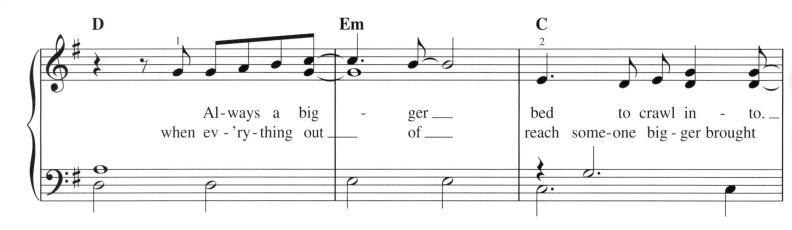

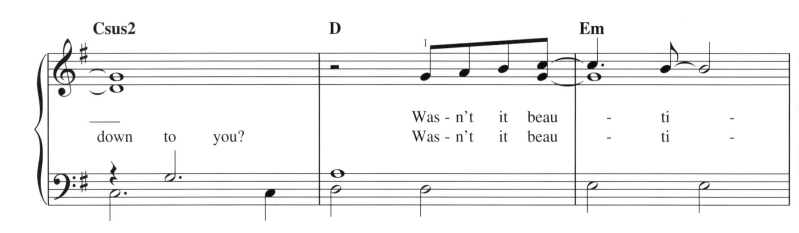

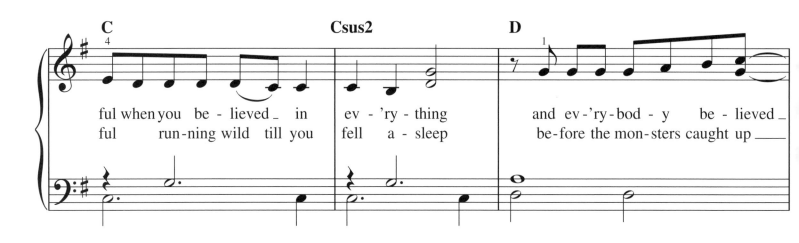

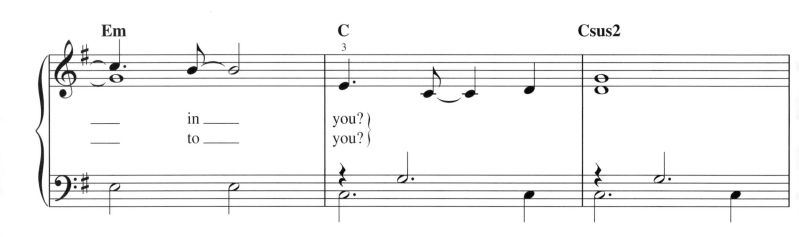

It's al - right, just ____ wait and see. Your string of lights is still ____

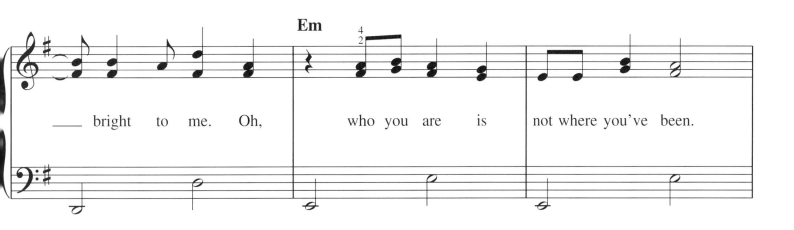

____ bright to me. Oh, who you are is not where you've been.

1.

You're still an in - no - cent. ____

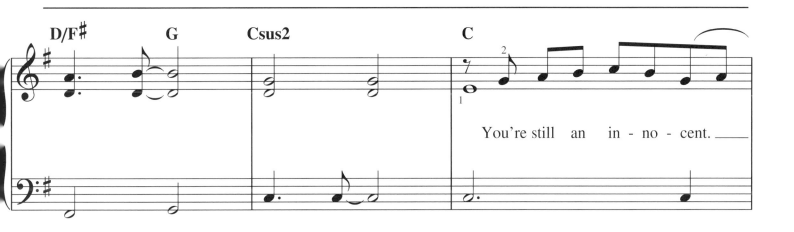

You're still an in - no - cent. ____

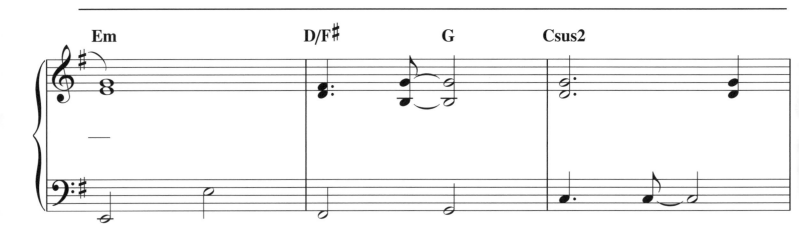

You're still an in - no - cent. It's o - kay, life _

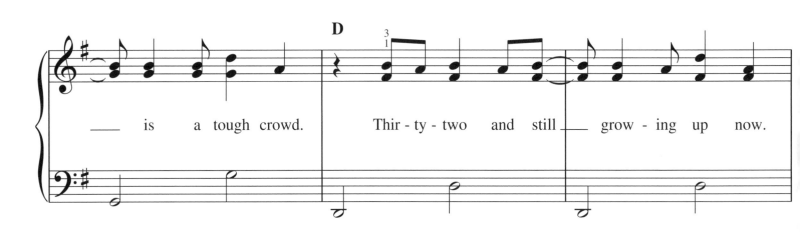

_ is a tough crowd. Thir - ty - two and still _ grow - ing up now.

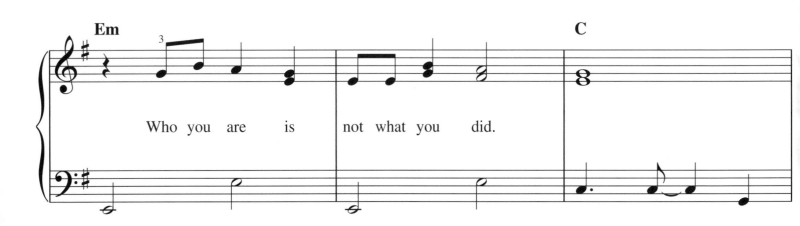

Who you are is not what you did.

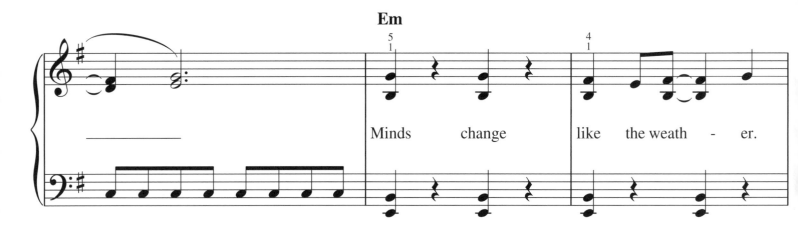

Minds change like the weath - er.

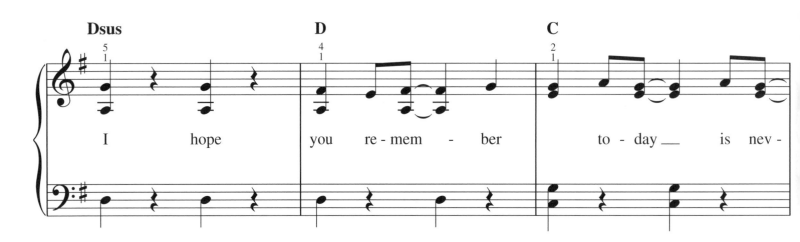

I hope you re - mem - ber to - day ___ is nev -

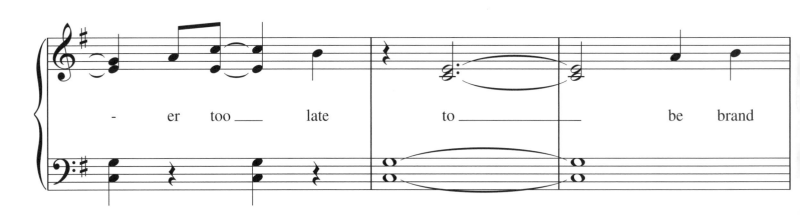

- er too ___ late to _____ be brand

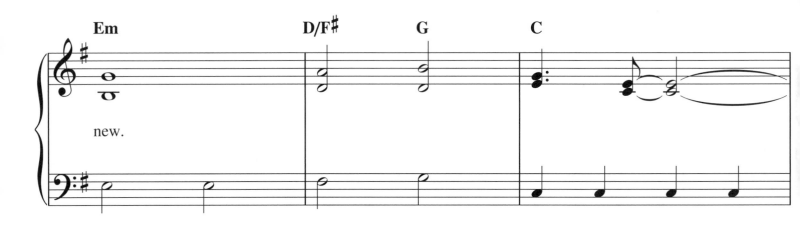

new.

HAUNTED

Words and Music by
TAYLOR SWIFT

Broadly, with epic feel

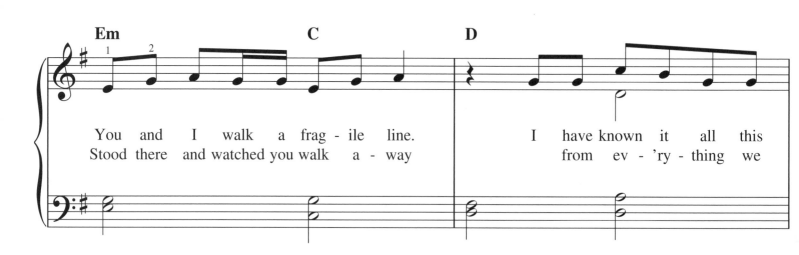

You and I walk a frag - ile line.   I have known it all this
Stood there and watched you walk a - way   from ev - 'ry - thing we

Copyright © 2010 Sony/ATV Music Publishing LLC and Taylor Swift Music
All Rights Administered by Sony/ATV Music Publishing LLC, 8 Music Square West, Nashville, TN 37203
International Copyright Secured All Rights Reserved

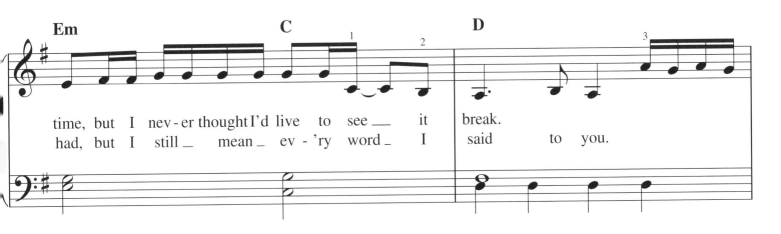

time, but I nev - er thought I'd live to see ___ it break.

had, but I still ___ mean ___ ev - 'ry word ___ I said to you.

It's get-ting dark and it's all so qui-et and I can't trust an - y - thing ___ now, and it's

He will try to take a - way my pain and he just ___ might ___ make me ___

com-ing o - ver you like it's all a big ___ mis - take.

smile, but the whole time I'm wish-ing he ___ was you in - stead.

Oh, ___ hold-ing my breath. Won't ___ lose you a - gain.

Oh, ___ hold-ing my breath, Won't ___ see you a - gain.

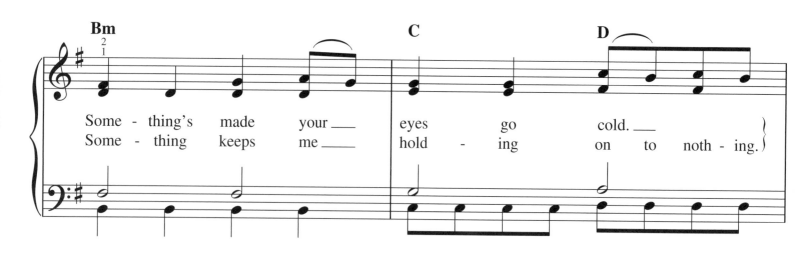

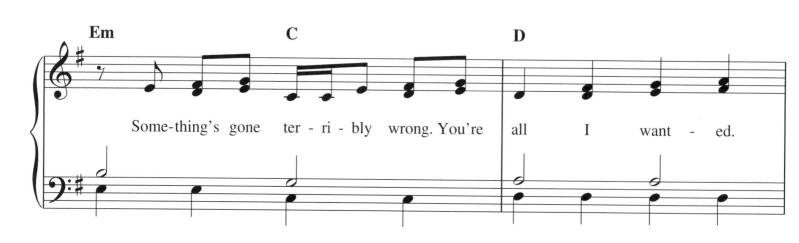

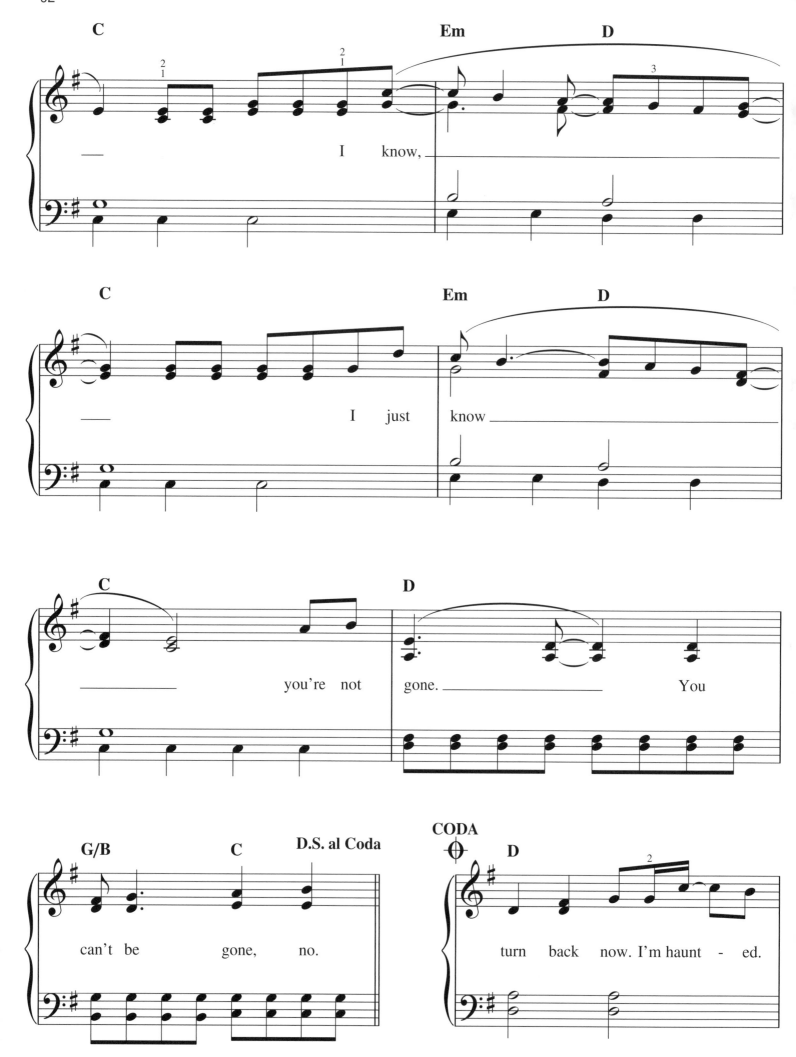

LAST KISS

Words and Music by
TAYLOR SWIFT

Moderately, in 2

With pedal

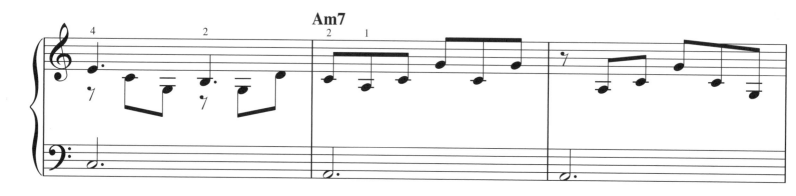

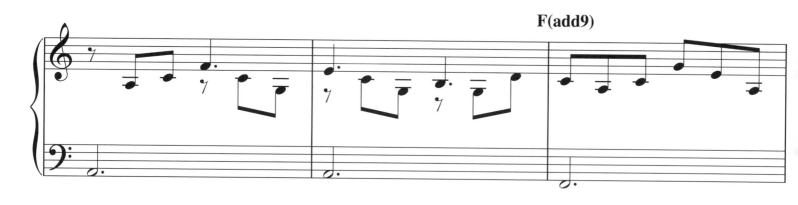

Copyright © 2010 Sony/ATV Music Publishing LLC and Taylor Swift Music
All Rights Administered by Sony/ATV Music Publishing LLC, 8 Music Square West, Nashville, TN 37203
International Copyright Secured   All Rights Reserved

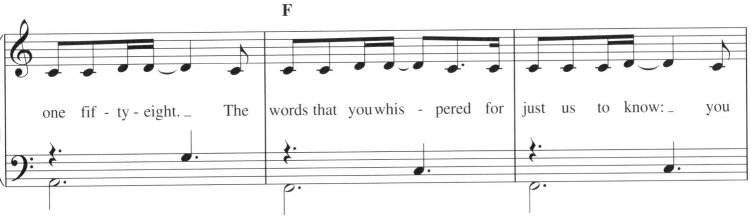

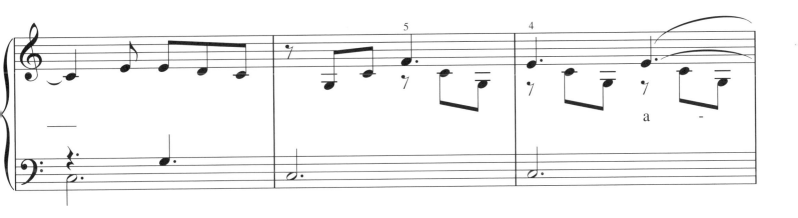

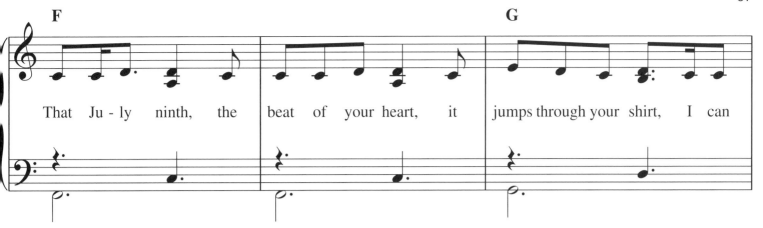

That Ju - ly ninth, the beat of your heart, it jumps through your shirt, I can

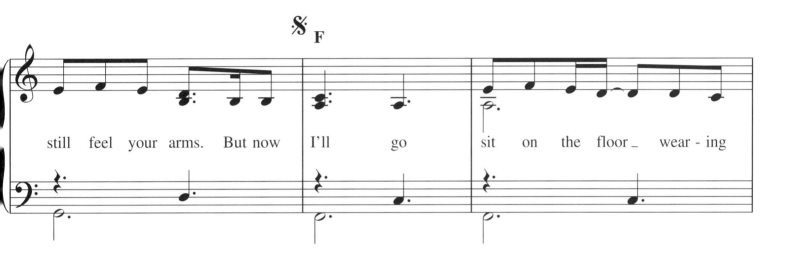

still feel your arms. But now I'll go sit on the floor wear - ing

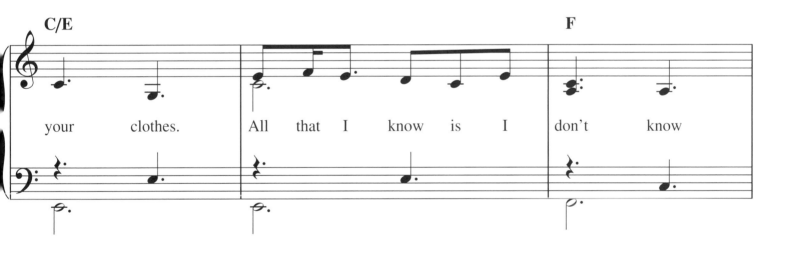

your clothes. All that I know is I don't know

how to be some-thing you miss. I nev - er thought we'd have a

last   kiss.

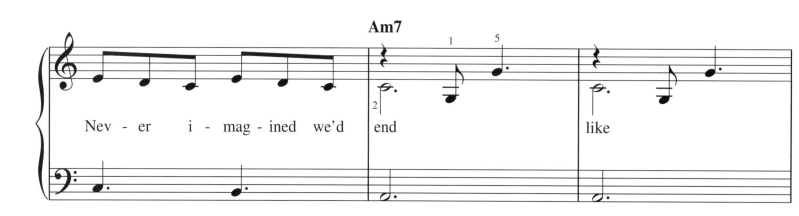

Am7

Nev - er   i - mag - ined we'd   end   like

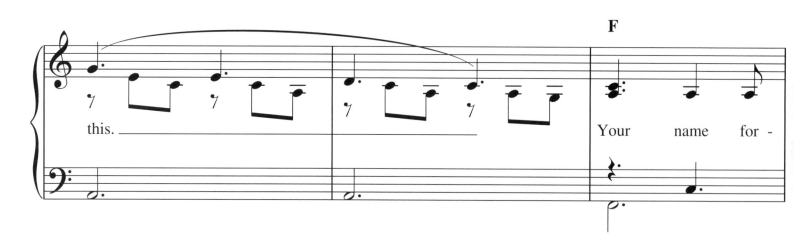

F

this. _____   Your   name   for -

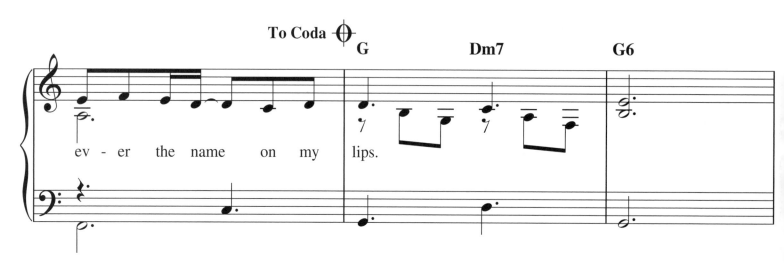

To Coda ⊕ **G**   **Dm7**   **G6**

ev - er the name   on my   lips.

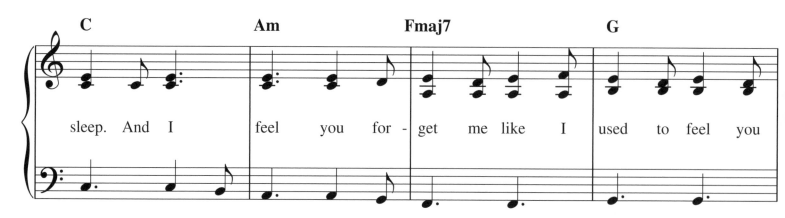

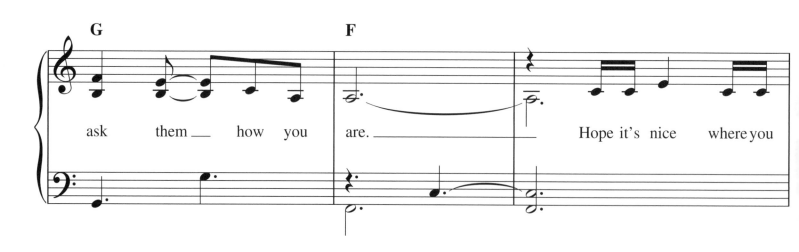

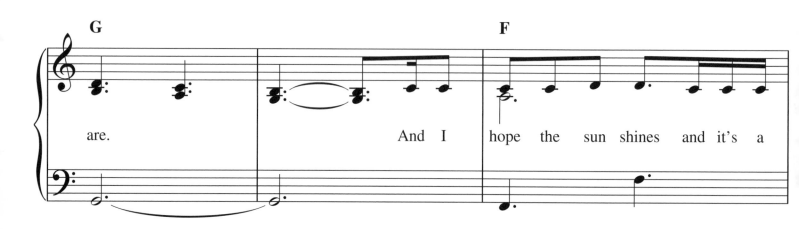

beau - ti - ful day and some - thing re - minds __ you you wish you had stayed. You can

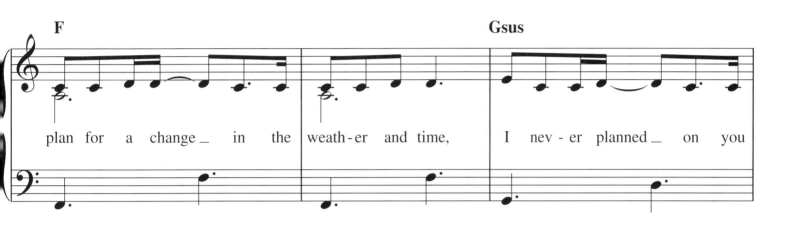

plan for a change __ in the weath - er and time, I nev - er planned __ on you

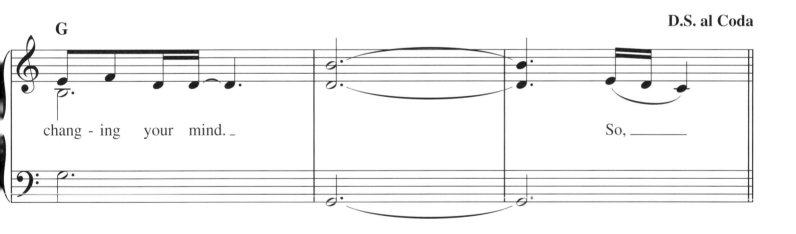

chang - ing your mind. __ So, _____

lips. Just like our last

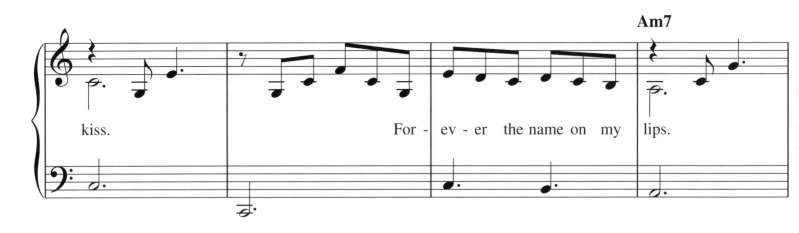

Additional Lyrics

I love your handshake, meeting my father.
I love how you walk with your hands in your pockets.
How you'd kiss me when I was in the middle of saying something.
There's not a day I don't miss those rude interruptions.

And I'll go sit on the floor...

LONG LIVE

Words and Music by
TAYLOR SWIFT

Copyright (c) 2010 Sony/ATV Music Publishing LLC and Taylor Swift Music
All Rights Administered by Sony/ATV Music Publishing LLC, 8 Music Square West, Nashville, TN 37203
International Copyright Secured   All Rights Reserved

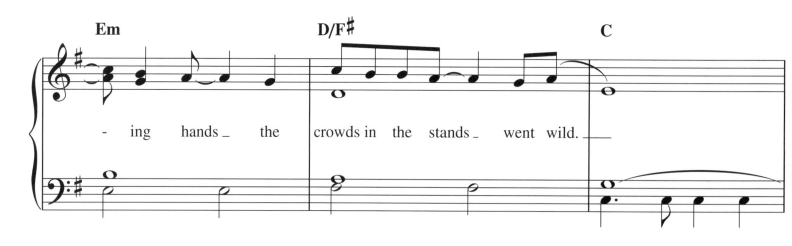

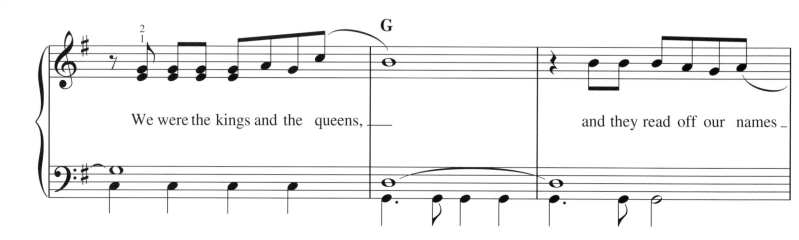

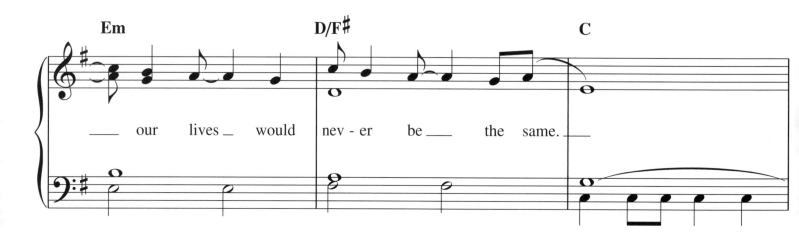

You held your head like a he - ro on a his-t'ry book page.

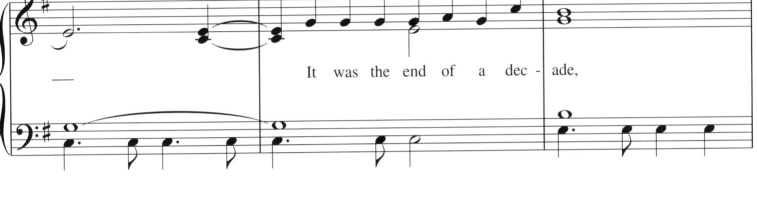

It was the end of a dec - ade,

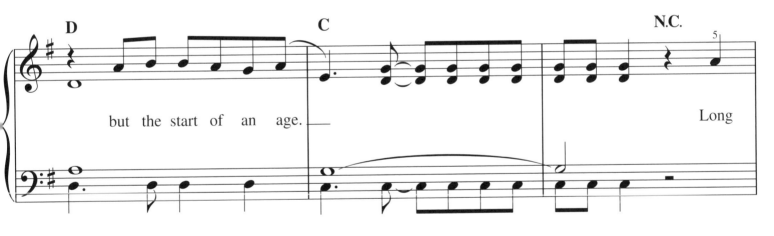

but the start of an age. Long

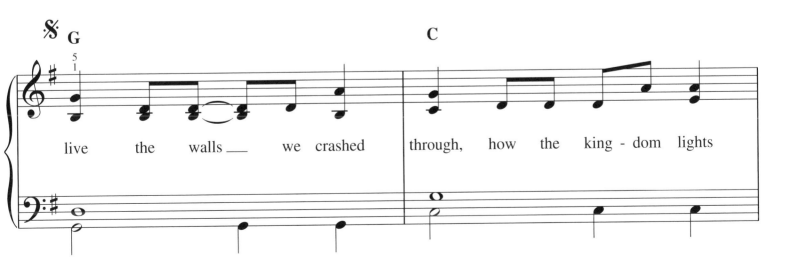

live the walls we crashed through, how the king - dom lights

in _____ and force us in-to a good-bye,

if you have chil-dren some-day, ___ when they point to the pic-

tures, please tell them my name. ___

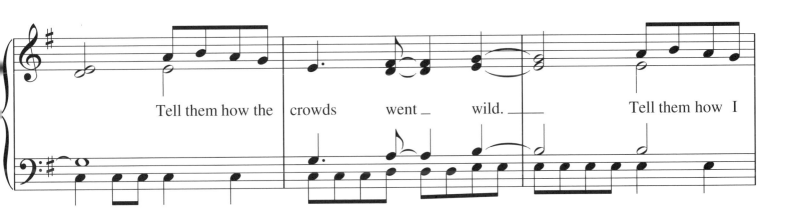

Tell them how the crowds went _ wild. ___ Tell them how I

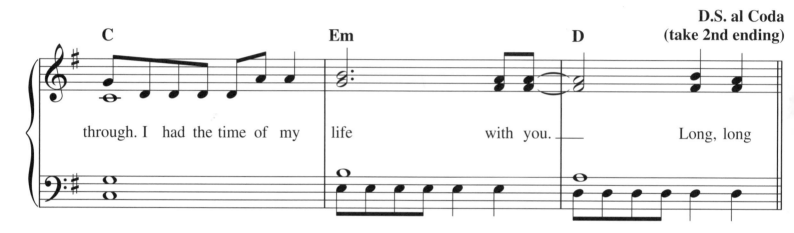

Additional Lyrics

2. I said remember this feeling.
   I pass the pictures around
   Of all the years that we stood there
   On the sidelines wishing for right now.
   We are the kings and the queens.
   You traded your baseball cap for a crown
   When they gave us our trophies
   And we held them up for our town.
   And the cynics were outraged,
   Screaming, "This is absurd."
   'Cause for a moment a band of thieves
   In ripped-up jeans got to rule the world.

   Long live the walls we crashed through...